The journey through grief c
face grief at some point in
stories of heartbreaking grie
finding meaning in your accomplishments, having rules to guide you, or realizing that you are not alone in your grief, this touching compilation is sure to inspire you not to give up.

Sarah McGillivray, B. Sc., M. Sc., A. Th. S., M. Ed., CCC, LCT

In <u>Stories of Good Grief</u> Tammy Leigh Robinson has invited a number of "every day" people to share their experiences of grief and how they worked through it. What is unique about this collection is that although grief was the cause of each story, hope became the overwhelming end result. The stories contained within this book are moments of authenticity and vulnerability. These dynamics serve to transform a reader's mere academic understanding of grief and hope to a more fully realized reality.

Reverend Ryan Farrell, B.A. Rel., M. Div.

Stories of

Good Grief

Tammy Leigh Robinson

ISBN 978-0-9958264-9-6
eBook ISBN 978-1-7389496-0-1
Cataloguing in Publication information available from Library and Archives
Canada

Copyright©2023 Tammy Leigh Robinson
TLR Publishing, Nackawic NB Canada
Published and printed in Canada
Visit www.TammyRobinsonAuthor.com

Cover design by The 905 Arts
sales@the905arts.com

Dedication

This book is dedicated to the loved ones mentioned herein who have passed on from this life. You are loved and missed dearly.

Never forgotten.

<u>Acknowledgements</u>

First and foremost, I thank my Heavenly Father for many things. Mostly I thank Him for always being with me, especially during times of grief. I also thank Him for giving me the creative idea to put this book together.

Secondly, I thank Granger E. Westberg for his book <u>Good Grief.</u> This book helped me so much when I was grieving at different times in my life. I've also shared this book with others who have found it helpful.

I also thank my husband, Keith, for editing the book. His encouragement and insight have meant so much to me. I'm so grateful to know you are always in my corner!

Finally, I thank all the people who have opened their hearts to share their story with us. Sometimes, it can be emotional when we talk about our grief, especially those who are dealing with ongoing grief. Thank you for being willing to face your feelings and share them with our readers. You are encouraging many people. Thank you!

Forward

What is grief?

Individual experiences of grief vary and are influenced by the nature of the loss. Some examples of loss include the death of a loved one, the ending of an important relationship, job loss, loss through theft or the loss of independence through disability.

Grief has physical, cognitive, behavioral, social, cultural, spiritual, and philosophical dimensions. In fact, individuals may find themselves feeling numb and removed from daily life, unable to carry on with regular duties while saddled with their sense of loss.

If you're uncertain about whether your grieving process is "normal," consult your health care professional. Outside help is sometimes beneficial when trying to recover and adjust to a death or diagnosis of a terminal illness.

Stories of Good Grief consists of 20 original stories, from 20 different individuals. Some of the stories were written by the contributing authors and others were told and written by the main author, Tammy Robinson.

The authors come from different backgrounds, ethnicity, age and spiritual beliefs. The one element they do share: grief.

You will read how they overcame the loss of a loved one, their mobility, their identity, their freedom. Cancer, suicide, war, homelessness, incarceration, fibromyalgia, and murder are some of the topics covered in this book.

The good news is the stories are meant to bring you HOPE - however YOU see that.

How you choose to read this book is your decision. Every chapter is that author's story. Perhaps, you may relate to one author and how they dealt with their grief.

We all experience grief during our life. Nobody should tell you how you are supposed to feel when grieving or that you need to "move on" with life. Grieving is a process and there may be times when everything seems impossible.

Please remember, you are not alone.

If you have ever flown, you would have been instructed on how to properly secure your oxygen mask. The flight attendant would have stressed to secure your own mask before helping someone else.

You need to take care of yourself first before helping others.

These authors have secured their (grief) mask and now, are ready to help YOU.

Finally, as I have been reading and editing this book, I have dealt with my own grief. My uncle passed away from a lengthy battle with Parkinsons while other family members continue their journey dealing with cancer and multiple sclerosis.

Another day ... another day sharing grief ....

Keith Robinson
CEO of TLR Publishing
co-editor of Stories of Good Grief

Table of Contents

Introduction:

One of the most important points about the 10 stages of grief is that they come in no particular order. Right behind that is the fact that just because you've experienced a stage of grief it doesn't mean you won't experience that stage again -in fact, you probably will.

Grief can be like waves in the ocean. They can come out of nowhere crashing down on you, sometimes knocking you off your feet and pushing you to the sandy bottom. At times they can completely overwhelm you. Thankfully, once they reach the crest, they lessen and usually peter out.

However, sometimes before it is gone, another wave comes crashing down on us. It may be the same stage or a different one. Sometimes we can experience more than one stage at the same time.

The important thing to remember as you read this book, whether you're grieving or want to know how to help your loved one who is grieving, is that every person is different, and every situation is different. While people and situations have similarities, they won't be exactly the same. So, let's not try to fit into a certain mold. Let's breathe deep and allow ourselves to process the stages of grief as they come.

Lastly, keep in mind that grief is defined as the natural reaction to loss. That loss can be any type of loss, from the loss of life of a close loved one to the loss of a job, business, relationship, or even the loss of our health. I personally know people who grieve the loss of being able to bare children.

Wikipidia states: *grief is the response to loss, particularly to the loss of someone or some living thing that has died, to which a bond or affection was formed.* Although conventionally focused on the emotional response to loss, grief also has physical, cognitive, behavioral, social, cultural, spiritual, and philosophical dimensions.

Our goal in this book is to aide you in processing your grief in a healthy manner. By sharing our stories of grief, sometimes in healthy manners and sometimes in not-so-healthy ways, we want to empower you to process your grief in the healthiest manner possible.

Ten Stages of Grief

The State of Shock

Expressing Emotion

Depression and Loneliness

Physical Symptoms

Panic and Overwhelm

Feelings of Guilt

Anger and Resentment

Resist Returning

Hope Comes Through

We Find a New Reality

The State of Shock. This is often the first stage people experience. Whether we were sidelined unexpectedly by the loss, or it was a long and dragged-out process, once the loss occurs it is often hard to believe it really happened. So much so, that our minds and our bodies just can't seem to process what has happened.

I liken this stage to the fight or flight or freeze reflex. It is a means our body uses to be able to cope during the grief. You'll often see this in a loving spouse at the funeral. He or she may show no trace of tears, and even be jovial. Inside they are devastated but their body knows it has certain duties to perform and so it separates the facts to work through the first difficult steps of the journey.

Another example is the person who just lost their job they've been at for over 20 years. They were hoping for a promotion, but they got cut instead. They are so overwhelmed they may walk around trance-like for hours, just trying to comprehend the magnitude of the loss.

One thing that seems to help people through this process is to keep busy. As much as possible continue to perform your normal activities. For example, if you have to pack to go home for the funeral, by all means have a friend or loved one with you but pack the suitcase yourself. Sometimes people mean well and want to do everything for you. That can do more harm than good. If you have nothing to do it is easier to slip into depression.

On the other hand, don't overdo it. As much as it is possible try to maintain a balance of activity. While it is not a good time to make major decisions, making small decisions, like to wear the red top instead of the blue one, will help to establish a sense of normalcy.

This stage can last anywhere from a few minutes to a few hours or days. If it lasts for weeks, it may become unhealthy and professional help should be sought out.

Expressing Emotion. Often about the time the shock wears off and the truth of our loss sinks in, we may feel an overwhelming sense of loss that comes bursting out of us. If we feel emotions, it is healthy to release them. One reason we have tear glands is because our bodies need to release emotions.

Sometimes men find this stage difficult because since they were young, they were told "Big boys don't cry." That sentence implies tears are seen as a sign of weakness. I put the thought to you that the opposite is true; tears are a sign of strength. Is it easy to cry in front of people? No, it is hard because you are vulnerable. It takes a *strong* person to cry.

Depression and Loneliness. Depression is deeper than sadness. It is like when there is a big black cloud over the sun. It looks like the sun isn't shining at all and the cloud looks like it is stuck. Sometimes it moves very slowly, but it will move, and we will see the sun shining again.

I like this quote by J. K. Rowling: "It's so difficult to describe depression to someone who's never been there, because it's not sadness. I know sadness. Sadness is to cry and to feel. But it's that cold absence of feeling—that really hollowed-out feeling."

Along with the awfulness of depression comes feelings of utter isolation. Sometimes it feels as if nobody has ever hurt like we're hurting. It's true –no two situations are exactly the same, but this is a time where we can take comfort in knowing we are not alone. Others have felt grief, depression, and loneliness too. This is one reason we're compiling our stories in this book.

Our hope is that in sharing our experience of grief with you that you will feel some encouragement. Remember: this stage will pass too.

Physical Symptoms. Working through grief is not easy. It is also not quick. It takes strength. Finding ways to manage your grief is of utmost importance.

Perhaps reading our stories will help you. Perhaps you find solace in meditation, yoga, prayer, music, poetry, or any number of healthy choices.

There are two keys to this point. 1: Healthy choices and 2: Do something.

So many people stop short of working through their grief and end up with some physical ailment years later. It can be anything from headaches and aches and pains to more serious things. It is our body's way of telling us that something is wrong. Many times, when patients see their doctors for symptoms and all tests are coming back negative, they eventually realize they've experienced a great loss in the past few months or years that hasn't been worked through.

Panic and Overwhelm. When grief is fresh it is hard to think of anything else. It is hard to concentrate, whether in reading or listening to someone speak or doing tasks at work. This is completely normal. Because the grief is so big in our life it can seem impossible to focus on anything else. Sometimes we just cannot imagine what our future will look like.

Here are some additional resources to look into:
https://www.mayoclinic.org/patient-visitor-guide/support-groups/what-is-grief

https://en.wikipedia.org/wiki/Grief

Grief can also cause us to panic and think worse-case-scenario in situations that we wouldn't normally think like that. Again, this is where the fight or flight or freeze response may be triggered. It is like our body is in a heightened state of anxiety. Sometimes it helps to gain knowledge about things like panic and learn what activities might help to ground us.

https://www.sciencedirect.com/science/article/abs/pii/S0005789419300826

One example is submersing our wrists under cold running water or splashing cold water on your face. It is like shocking your body into stepping back from the intensity of emotion and taking a new look at the facts of the situation. It can also help to take three deep belly breathes in through the nose, hold it for about three or four seconds and release it slowly through your mouth.

It also helps if we have someone as an emergency contact that can help walk you through the situation with grounding questions. You can also write out your grounding questions so you can work through it yourself. For example, you can ask yourself "What is the worst-case scenario?" Then answer that question. "What would you do if... (worst-case scenario) happened?" When you can answer that and realize that the worst-case scenario is most likely not going to happen, it can encourage you that whatever the facts of the situation truly are, you will be able to manage the situation.

In an article by Science Direct (Behavior Therapy Volume 51, Issue 3, 2020, Pages 413-423) it was stated that 91.4% of people's worries do not come true, for people with GAD (Generalized Anxiety Disorder). That percentage would be even higher for people who do not have GAD.

Feelings of Guilt. For me personally I found this stage one of the most difficult to deal with. Again, each situation is different, AND it is quite normal for people who are grieving to say or think, "If only I had..." or the opposite; "If only I hadn't..."

It is important to realize there is a "normal" guilt and an unhealthy guilt. A normal guilt would be having said something in an argument with someone that is not truly how you feel. Later you apologize for what you said in the heat of the moment. However, an unhealthy guilt would be if that person suddenly died and you blamed yourself for their death, thinking, "If I hadn't said that they would still be alive."

Or the mother whose child is on their death bed. They've spent days at their bedside without sleep. The doctor convinces the parent to go home and get some sleep. While the parent is gone the child takes a turn for the worse and passes away. The parent will probably be sad and wish she had been at her child's bedside, but if she blames herself to the point that she feels if she had stayed at the bedside the child would still be alive that would be unhealthy. Likewise, if she becomes obsessed with the sadness from not being there at the time of death that could be unhealthy.

The harsh truth is what is done, is done, and cannot be changed by asking "what if?" We're not discounting the fact that we can use every situation in life as a learning opportunity to become stronger and better people. We are addressing the heavy guilt that makes you think your loss is because of something you did or didn't do. As they say, "Don't drink that Kool-Aid." Your feelings of guilt may prevent you from working through your grief. The more you can keep your thoughts on the current situation and hopes of the future instead of the past the healthier your grief will be. Though, during grief it can be extremely difficult to see any hope in the future.

Anger and Resentment. These feelings are also "normal" human emotions. When we get to the point that we accept our loss it can be natural to feel angry about it. The anger may be directed at someone involved, like a doctor or the new boss, or it may even be directed at God. "Why did God let this happen?" That is close to the age-old question, "Why do bad things happen to good people?" That is a subject for another book.

With this book, we want to look at healthy ways of expressing our anger. Sometimes anger can be misdirected to someone or over something that has nothing to do with the loss. For example, after the loss of someone in your immediate family you go to the store to buy an outfit for the funeral. The salesperson charges you the wrong price and you over-react. Had the same thing happened six months earlier you wouldn't have been so hostile.

One way of finding release from anger is journaling. It may sound counter productive. Why would you want to record your awful feelings? It is the act of releasing the feelings from inside you to outside of you and onto the paper that makes this a healthy action. You may even want to burn the journal later. Or maybe if we're sincerely blaming someone, perhaps a drunk driver hit and killed our loved one, we can write a letter to them to get out all the anger and resentment. Instead of mailing the letter we can burn it.

Although it is difficult to deal with anger, it is imperative that it be dealt with. If it is left alone, it won't just go away. It will fester into resentment. Many people become bitter with resentment over loss that wasn't dealt with. Please don't let that be your story.

Resist Returning. This stage is a real balancing act. In our western, modern society it almost seems as if grief isn't allowed. History tells us people would wear black or say certain prayers for months to acknowledge their grief. Now it seems like once the funeral is finished it is back to normal. The problem is that the person with the loss must now find a new normal. If it is a loss of a job, the person now must start looking for a new job. In the case of a death, there is a void in everyday life for the ones left here on earth.

Many times, friends and family think they cannot bring up anything about the person who passed away because it might re-open the wound. In truth, the grieving person is already thinking about their loved one. Hearing a funny story about the person, or even a feel-good story about them can bring healing. Too often we feel like our loved one is forgotten about.

On the other hand, sometimes, people just won't let the loved one go. Years later you visit the grieving person, and you can't have a conversation without them bringing up the person and how much their lives have changed because of their death.

Please don't get me wrong. For sure talk about them if that is the normal course of the conversation, but if they are in every conversation and if it is always in reference to how hard life is without them, then this could signify an unhealthy situation.

Hope Comes Through. This stage can be a catch 22. We may be in the midst of deep grief for many weeks, or even months. Nobody knows how long grief will last. As we already mentioned grief can be different for different people and in different situations.

It also bears reminding that some people may not go through every stage. Some people may not express emotion because that is the type of person they are. Or perhaps they don't feel the anger because they secretly hated the job they lost or their loved one was suffering in pain, and they're relieved to know they aren't suffering anymore.

At some point the dark clouds of grief will start to break up and HOPE will come streaming through. Even when that happens, we may find ourselves with waves of guilt upon us again as we realize we're looking forward to something coming up soon when we just buried our loved one a few months ago. We may mistakenly feel we should never or will never be happy again.

The main point we want you to take away from this book is the fact that grief is difficult, and it can be managed. Lean on your support network to help you through this time. If you have a broken leg you use the support of crutches, right? So, when you're grieving lean into your support resources.

We Find a New Reality. Notice we didn't say "we go back to reality". Our lives are forever changed by this loss. The trajectory of our path in life has changed. I often say, "I had to find a 'new normal' because I would never be able to have my old normal again."

Grief changes us. We are not the same person after a huge loss. We're either stronger for it and can encourage others through our grief or we become weaker and may not be the fulfilled member of society we were or could be.

Some people's faith is deepened, or they find faith when they didn't have faith. Some people give up on their faith. Our hope for you as you delve into this book is that you will be encouraged by our stories. Learn what things helped us and what things made a bad situation worse.

Our other hope for you is that some day you will be able to encourage someone else by sharing your story of grief with them.

I'd also like to invite you to share your story with me. At some point there may be a second Stories of Good Grief book. You can email your story to me at: admin@TammyRobinsonAuthor.com.

For more information, read Good Grief by Granger E. Westberg

A Different Kind of Grief

Written as told by Geneva Coach G Livingstone

Geneva is an Emotional Luxury Coach. She helps people discover a different type of grief. She offers a loving and kind approach to dealing with grief.

Within a 22-month period Geneva had a cousin die, her 25-year-old son died, then another cousin died. Her family experienced 3 children's deaths in that short timeframe.

When she first got into coaching she was hesitant in getting into grief counselling because it felt a bit like selling a story. Friends kept telling her she needed to say something about grief because sometimes the way people treat you in your grief is brutal.

Most of the time people don't know how they should treat people who are grieving. So, Geneva came up with the concept of "death etiquette". She shot a video about it the day after her son's birthday.

Death etiquette talks about how to support a griever as well as how the griever can support themselves within their community by having a voice. Once grief hits, you begin to hear stories of what other people have gone through.

Geneva previously contributed to a book entitled <u>Good Grief</u>. She talked about how to support grievers. Her chapter wasn't only from her but was also from other people who had experienced grief. It talked about how they were treated at the most tender time in their lives.

When she thinks of grief now, she thinks not only of how the griever is processing their grief, but also how do they allow themselves to be treated by others. She cares so much about that.

It can seem like people lose their identity when they are grieving. So many times, people are treated like they aren't adults and can't make decisions for themselves. The griever can feel like saying, "Woe! You need to back up!" So often the griever doesn't feel like they can voice when they're feeling like this.

This is what her grief work is about now. Rather than it being focused on what she went through in her own grief, she focuses on helping others process their grief. We all grieve differently. Geneva's grief was extremely different from what she has heard from a lot of people about their grief when they lost a child.

Most people are devastated and feel hollow. They often feel like they are only surviving because of the children they have left, instead of really getting into how they are feeling.

It was when she was going through this that she realized grief is like a rupture of a volcano that pulls everything in your life to the surface at one time. So, not only are you dealing with grief, but you're also dealing with all the other stuff you haven't dealt with.

She questioned, "Why am I not like this? How come I grieve differently? What's happening? Something is wrong with me. Am I ignoring it? What is going on?"

She realized she wasn't ignoring it. Her emotional quotient (EQ) was very high. Unfortunately, a lot of people don't have that high EQ so the weight of grief really takes their feet out from under them. Out of 100, the tipping point is about 75%.

A year-and-a-half after her son died, her EQ was at an 86, meaning she was above what most people are. That calmed her judgements in her mind because she was no longer looking at herself, wondering what was wrong with her. She no longer wondered if she didn't love her child enough. She no longer wondered if she didn't experience her son well enough, or was she in shock, or was she lying. Her EQ answered all of those questions.

That's when she realized we need to talk about emotional intelligence. We need to talk about emotional luxury in the heart of the griever. She has encountered people as low as 11%. Now, she understood why they felt lost.

When she works with people who have a low EQ she approaches it differently than someone with a high EQ. It makes sense of how they feel.

The other assessment that she does is called the Saboteur Assessment which comes from the book Positive Intelligence by Shirzad Chamine. When the mental saboteurs pop up Geneva can understand what voices are talking to the griever other than their own. Everything comes up.

For example, when a man who starts drinking when grieving the death of his child, we may say "Oh, he's self-medicating." Now we realize there is a reason for it. Let's take his EQ and see what his saboteurs are so we can work with them and help him level out and balance it.

Being an Emotional Luxury Coach, Geneva doesn't only help with grief. As we know grief is not only the loss of a loved one. It is essentially the loss of anything important to us.

She helped a woman in her 60's deal with her grief of being molested by a nun. Imagine carrying that her whole life. It wasn't because she didn't say something. It was because she wasn't seen, heard, or validated. Geneva's work was to be with her client in that moment and to hear her, to let her speak and have her own voice.

This woman had just lost her brother. Because she's already dealt with the past, she can grieve her brother in the here and now. It is beautiful to be able to function in the now instead of being caught up in the past. She can grieve differently because she's dealt with the past.

When asked what grief was like in Geneva's experience, she said it was a shock. Her cousin was a healthy 51-year-old who went to the hospital for severe back pain and never came out. It was a problem with his kidney.

Likewise, her son went to the hospital for an asthma attack and didn't come out. One lung collapsed, then the other collapsed. She didn't think, "What am I going to do?" because that isn't the type of person she is. She was able to be glad that her son passed away before Covid started.

He was 25 years old when he died. Geneva didn't feel she could be lost in her own space because her son's lifetime friends needed comforting, as well as her family. She felt she really needed to hold the space for a lot of people until they left. Then she cried.

She still has a daughter and a mom who were grieving. Geneva had to watch her mom say goodbye to her grandchild. "I made sure everyone else was okay."

She described her grief as active because she stayed busy. Four months prior to her son's death she had started her coaching program. Her son had said, "Mom, you should be a counsellor. Everyone listens to you when you talk!"

When her cousin passed, Geneva got angry with death. She said, "Death and I were going to have a fight." She started an Instagram account and posted many things about the types of grief. Then she started going live online to talk about grief and to provide a place for people to talk and share their stories.

It helped those who were feeling alone and isolated in their grief. Geneva said she didn't feel that way in her grief, but she realized that many people do.

One aspect of Geneva's coaching is to help people be heard. However, some people don't want to speak. They need to be seen and acknowledged. For those who don't want to talk, or are tired of talking, their feelings still need to be validated.

The support comes from encouraging clients to create their own support system so that they are not exhausting the person beside them, who is also grieving, which we have a tendency to do because we don't know better.

Instead of expecting every person in your life to hold that space for you, they can have that support person who they can have coffee with, even six months to two years later. This is where they can still say the name of their child, or their dad, or whoever had died.

People can connect directly with Geneva on Facebook messenger at GenevaCoachgLivingstone or

https://m.me/geneva.coachg.livingstone.

Geneva wants every grieving heart to understand that you do have a voice. You do get to decide how other people treat you. You do get to "open" or "close" your space as you see fit. You are capable even if it feels like you're not capable right now.

To "open" your space is to accept people into your space, life, and experience. It can be a cultural thing where everybody shows up to your house even if you're not ready for visitors. You can feel like you must perform when you'd rather just be with your family. To "close" your space is to say to a person, "No, I don't feel like having a visitor."

When people show up you don't have to answer your door. Or you can say,

"Today is not a good day," If you want to stay in your pajamas, you can. Then, when you're ready to open your space, you can invite people in. Also, when you're ready to open your space, you can choose who you open to -it doesn't have to be everybody.

This gives the power back to the griever. This is why the building of a tribe, or a community around you is so important. It can be three or four different friends. It is helpful. You might have a friend who will sit on the couch and let you cry everything out and not even talk or wipe your tears -just let you cry it out.

You might have an active friend who will take you to dinner or take the kids so you can cry and be on your own. You might have another friend who makes you laugh. So when you want to laugh you call that person and they help you laugh because that's exactly what that person's role is. You choose these people and ask them if they will fill that role. These people become your core support system.

Geneva had a woman whose husband died. There was a lot of paperwork to be done and every time she had to repeat her story. She was feeling overwhelmed. Then Geneva asked her if she had a really good friend that she could entrust this task to. The woman said yes, she did have a friend who could fill this role. So, her friend would tell her story for her, and she would show up on the call to do the final details. This way she didn't have to keep going over her husband's passing repeatedly -it is not fair.

Many times when people ask what happened, they aren't asking for you but for their own curiosity. Therefore, they aren't in that space to help you. As a griever you need people who are in your space for you. So, having those friends around you is super important. It allows you to be protected.

When asked if she could go back in time to say something to her grieving self when her son died, she said she would give her a big hug and say, "You're going to be okay! You're going to be amazing!"

Again, at that time, she thought something was wrong with her because she really was okay. She even tried to close herself off for a day and she truly felt she didn't need that separation.

Grief was different for her than most people. Looking back, she understands why she felt okay. She knows she can coach people in grief because she went through it in a way that reveals the underbelly that grief exposes. She also said she had an incredible net of people to support her.

Geneva added, the most important things are your voice and that you build a community of support for yourself on your terms. Grief shows up in so many different ways -not only in the death of a loved one. Many people experienced grief as children and it hasn't been dealt with.

Dealing with grief in this way really empowers people. And, remember if you're doing okay, that's good too. There's nothing wrong with you. You don't have to judge yourself and think you didn't love the person who died because you're doing okay.

Author Bio: Geneva Coach G Livingstone

Geneva Coach G Livingstone is a compressed grief survivor!! This means that in a period of 22 months her family lost 3 beautiful souls. All of them aged children including her own 25-year-old son Nathaniel.

Even though grief was not her original path to follow, the loss of her cousin (death #3) was enough to ignite a fire in her soul to start being a voice within the grief space.

It began with Death Etiquette on how to PROPERLY support a griever followed by becoming a certified Master Grief & Life Coach to adding The Confident Grief Coach certification and lastly being an Emotional Intelligence Practitioner.

With this specialized training, coupled with her 25 plus years in coaching, training and developing teams all of her experience has lead to focusing her heart in helping grievers.

Geneva has refined her message and has deepened her vision by recognizing how grief is truly steeped in layers.

It might have started off with just trying to help those who have lost someone dear to truly recognizing that grief is not just about the loss of a loved one BUT it's about the loss of ANYTHING that's important to you!!

It's now on this premise that Geneva bases her work and her brand Emotional Luxury because being SEEN, being HEARD and being VALIDATED are the right of every heart.

Geneva can be reached at: Theemotionalgazillionaire@gmail.com or on messenger at: https://m.me/geneva.coachg.livingstone.

Turning Life's Lemons Into Lemonade

Written by Tammy Allen

There's a saying that says, "When life hands you lemons, make lemonade." That's exactly what I learned to do. I went from being a vibrant young woman who wanted to spend my life in a foreign country as a missionary, to being in a wheelchair, living in a nursing home.

I felt like the female version of Job in the Bible. Job was a God-fearing man and he was very wealthy. He had all the earthly goods a person could want. His family was blessed, his business was blessed. Everything he put his hand to was blessed. Over a short period of time, he lost almost everything in his life.

Through many disasters, he lost his children, his livestock, his farm and employees and many other things in his life. The last thing he lost was his health. Almost overnight, he went from being healthy and wealthy, without a care in the world, to having lost almost everything and having a very painful disease in his body.

He went through a significant amount of grief. The only thing he had left in his life was his wife and a few friends. These people only added to his grief. His three friends accused Job of many things, telling him, that he lost everything because there was sin in his life. That was the farthest thing from the truth because the Bible says that there was none on earth as righteous as Job.

His friends were constantly blaming him for all his loss. Even during all his loss, Job never blamed God for it. He still trusted God through it all. The good news is, by the end of Job's life, he was blessed with twice as much as he previously had. Before God blessed Job, he had to learn to forgive those who blamed him for his loss and saying all those grievous things. Once he prayed for, what I would call his "frienemies," it was then that God blessed him with double.

I grew up healthy. The only illnesses I dealt with as a child was chicken pox, measles, and pneumonia. Other than that, I was pretty healthy. I grew up unaware of the physical trauma I was going to have to endure as a young adult.

When I was 14 I became a Christian. A few years after becoming a Christian, I had a desire to be a missionary. I had a heart for the less fortunate and I still do. As I got older, I did local outreaches to the homeless in my city. I also went to Bible school and mission school to get the training I needed. I had been on a couple of short-term mission trips, one of which I went on in the early stages of the disease I was diagnosed with.

I went through a lot of loss and grief in my life. What I'm about to share is one of the hardest things I've had to endure. When I was in my early twenties, I noticed my legs were slowly getting weak. It was getting hard to walk in high heels. I got muscle fatigue when I climbed stairs. I went several years like this. I went through a year of pain all throughout my body before going to see a doctor about it. I was also tripping over cracks in the sidewalks. I didn't go to the doctor about the pain for about a year because I thought the pain was because I did a lot of walking on my job. When I started tripping and falling, I decided to see a doctor about it. This was the beginning of a five-and-a-half-year journey of going through many medical tests to try and diagnose me.

In the beginning of going through medical tests, the specialists were testing me for the more common diseases. Every time a doctor would mention a disease, they were testing me for, I would go on the internet to learn more about the disease. They crossed all the common diseases off the list of possible diseases I could have had. It was a scary time for me because I didn't know what was wrong with me and I didn't know my prognosis. I didn't know if I was going to live or die.

I went through many medical tests during those five-and-a-half-years. Many times, I had to go to a hospital in London for tests. London was a couple hours away from my house. My dad drove me to all my appointments out of town. When we had to go to the hospital in London, we had to leave very early in the morning, spend the day at the hospital and then wouldn't get home until late in the evening. By the end of the day, I was worn out and in pain from all the medical tests I was put through. I was beginning to feel like a pin cushion or a science project. Some of the tests were painful. I was already dealing with pain from this unknown disease. On top of that, I had to deal with pain from the medical tests.

The following are some of the tests I went through, just to name a few. I had an EMG done several times. I had an MRI of my whole body, several CT scans. I had four biopsies, two were muscle biopsies, one was a skin biopsy and the last one was a nerve biopsy near my ankle.

When I had the nerve biopsy done, I wasn't in a wheelchair yet. The nerve biopsy was so painful that I couldn't walk for a week, so I had to use a wheelchair for that week. I had a bone scan, and lots of blood work. The doctor also did tests on my muscle strength. These were just some of the tests. There were too many to name them all. The tests all showed there was something wrong, but the specialists were having a hard time pinpointing what disease it was.

It was hard living in the unknown. I just wanted to get a diagnosis so I could know what was wrong and learn to deal with it.

Early on, in the beginning of all the tests, I was diagnosed with a severe case of fibromyalgia. The pain was so bad at times that it hurt for

23

people to even give me a hug. I am an affectionate person, but I dreaded when certain people hugged me because they hugged me too hard and it would cause me pain. The specialist who diagnosed me with fibromyalgia said that diagnosis was the least of his concerns. He said there was something a lot worse that was causing my other physical issues that were not consistent with fibromyalgia. He said, even though he diagnosed me with fibromyalgia, I needed to get further tests done to find out what the other disease was. After five-and-a-half-years of many long days of going through medical tests, I was diagnosed with Hereditary Inclusion Body Myopathy 2.

Back when I was diagnosed with Hereditary Inclusion Body Myopathy 2, there were only about five hundred people in the world with this disease. Since then, they have renamed the disease. It's now called GNE Myopathy. There are now a few thousand people in the world with the disease. The disease affects all the skeletal muscles. In most cases, the disease hits a person when they are in their twenties, but it's also known to hit other age groups. When I got diagnosed, the doctor said I would eventually end up in a wheelchair. People with the disease slowly lose their skeletal muscles.

I was devastated when I got diagnosed and found out I would permanently end up in a wheelchair. At the time of diagnosis, I could still walk without a mobility aid. I was very involved in my church. I was part of the choir and I volunteered in the church nursery. I also did a lot of outreaches in my city as well as in Michigan. It was very hard to deal with the idea of ending up in a wheelchair. I was supposed to become a missionary, and now I'm being told, I was going to slowly lose my muscle strength and end up in a wheelchair. When I got diagnosed, there wasn't much information out there about the disease. Since the disease hadn't been around for very long, and it was so rare, it was considered an orphan disease.

Being diagnosed with a crippling disease was a major test of my faith. I was trying to figure out what I did wrong to end up with this disease. Some other believers talked to me the way Job's friends spoke to him. Some said I had the disease because there was sin in my life, or I must be lacking faith. They would say if I had more faith I would be healed.

I couldn't figure out what I had done wrong. I eventually realized I did nothing to deserve the disease; it's just an unfortunate thing that happened.

Some people, like I did, automatically think they did something wrong, or God is mad at them when they end up sick or with a disease, or even when something negative happens in their life. This is untrue. God is our loving Heavenly Father, and He would never put sickness or disease on people.

In the early years of the disease, I was depressed because of my prognosis. I felt like, because of the disease and me eventually being in a wheelchair, I would be useless and would be just a waste of space on the earth. I felt like I would be better off in heaven than on earth. I felt like I would be of no use to God and would be a burden on people. I dreaded the thought of losing my independence. I was used to doing things by myself without having to depend on others. All these negative thoughts were going on in my head. People around me didn't know the inner turmoil I was going through. I was listening to too much of what others, who didn't know any better, were saying to me. It took awhile for me to get over the initial shock of my diagnosis.

In the earlier years of the disease, I tried everything in my own strength to get healed of the disease. I thought if I prayed a little harder or went on a fast God would heal me. I repented of every sin I could think of and forgave every person that I felt I had a grudge against. I wanted everything out of my life that I thought was hindering me from receiving my healing.

There weren't any major areas of sin in my life that I could think of, but just in case there was, I repented of it and asked God to forgive me. I changed my eating habits, and I went on long walks to try and get more muscle strength. I was getting frustrated because no matter what I did nothing was changing. Instead of getting better, things were only getting worse.

One day while praying, the Lord told me of a verse in Ephesians that said, "... having done all to stand. Stand therefore..." This verse is found in Ephesians 6:13, (KJV) the latter part and the beginning of verse 14. I had done "all," now it was my time to stand and leave it in God's hands. God didn't want me to struggle with it anymore. What He wanted, was for me to give it over to Him, trusting Him and not to strive anymore.

The more I prayed about it and studied the Bible, I realized what I was being told wasn't accurate. God is a good God. He would never put sickness or disease on someone. Any earthly parent would never inflict pain on their child or make their child sick to teach them a lesson. That would be considered child abuse. God would never abuse His children. Just because someone is sick or going through something, it doesn't automatically mean that they are lacking faith or in sin.

That may be true in some cases, but more often than not, it isn't true. One time, during worship, I was thinking about all of this and the Lord asked me what takes more faith. It's easy to have faith and live for God when our bodies are healthy and pain free and our bank accounts are full. It takes more faith to live for God when we are in pain and going through things.

God does not want us to be sick or in pain or broke; that's not His will. But it doesn't necessarily mean we are lacking faith if we are sick or broke. It's easy to trust God when things are going great; it's a choice we make to trust Him when things aren't going so great. It takes faith to pray for others' healing, while we are still believing for our own healing. It takes faith to get up and sing God's praises when things are going wrong in our lives.

As I spent more time praying and studying the word of God, my thinking changed. I no longer felt that it was the end of the world because of me being diagnosed with the disease. My future no longer looked dark. I am still the same person I was before I ended up in a wheelchair. I use this as an opportunity to minister to others who are dealing with disabilities, to be an encouragement to them. I tell them that it's not the end of the world and they are still an important part of society. People with disabilities are more willing to listen to me because I am in the same situation as them and I understand what they're going through.

As the disease progressed, I had to start using a cane. At first, I was too embarrassed to use a cane because I felt canes were for people much older than me. The only way my dad could get me to use anything that resembled a cane, was that he bought me an umbrella that had a cane like handle. He put a rubber thing on the metal part that touched the ground so it wouldn't slip.

So, there I was, limping around town, using a closed umbrella, as a cane, in bright sunlight, to try to keep me from falling. Looking back, I laugh at how silly I must have looked. I looked sillier with the umbrella than I would have with a cane. Eventually I did start using a cane and as the disease progressed, I started using a walker. I didn't use the walker much because it put pressure on my back and caused pain when I used it. Many years later I had to start using a wheelchair. At first, I only used the wheelchair when I was outdoors. While I was indoors, I used a cane. That didn't last long. Then, the thing I dreaded happened. I ended up having to permanently be in a wheelchair.

I came to realize that being in a wheelchair doesn't define who I am. I am still the same person I was before I ended up in a wheelchair. I no longer think I'm useless. I can do what most others can do; I just have to do it differently. I have a saying, "if you find you can no longer do something, do it differently."

As the disease progressed, and I lost the ability to do things, I would have to figure out a different way of doing it. I tried to keep my independence as long as I could. There were some things I would completely lose the ability to do, and I would go through my grieving period and then move on.

It's completely normal to go through the grieving process, when experiencing loss, whether it is the passing of a loved one, or a divorce, or being diagnosed with a disease, whatever it may be. God gave us tears for a reason. Even Jesus wept when He lost His good friend. It's important to allow yourself to go through the grieving process. Bottling it up and not going through the grieving process can be harmful. Allow yourself to go through the grieving process, but don't grieve to the point where it leads to depression.

The grieving process is different for everyone. For some it's longer and others it's shorter. Some people need counselling. I went to see a counsellor many times during my grieving process. Ecclesiastes 3:1 says, "To everything there is a season, and a time to every purpose under Heaven." (KJV) Then in verse 4 it goes on to say, "A time to weep, and a time to laugh. A time to mourn, and a time to dance."

For most of the early stages of the disease, even while in the wheelchair, I lived on my own. Eventually, as the disease progressed and I was unable to take care of myself, I had to move into a nursing home. I dreaded the thought of moving into a nursing home because I would have to depend on others to do most things for me. I got to the point where I could no longer do simple things like dress myself, wash my hair, bathe, brush my hair, wash my face. I had to depend on others to do it for me. It was very hard to give up my independence. Ending up in a nursing home was the hardest part of the disease process I've had to go through.

While living in the nursing home, as the disease progressed, I fell into a depression. This was the hardest part of the grieving process for me. I was depressed and lonely. I was losing the ability to do many things that I enjoyed, like playing the keyboard and I had to depend on others more and more.

My physical strength was declining fast. I had to deal with more physical issues. I was focusing on what I couldn't do instead of focusing on what I could still do. If I thought on the negative, I had feelings of depression. I had to change my thinking. I couldn't change what was happening to me, but I could change how I responded to it. I had to make a choice. Was I going to accept defeat or was I going to be an overcomer?

I heard a saying that goes something like this, "Life is 10% of what happens to us, and 90% of how we respond to the 10%." There were many things I could still do. As I got my focus off the negative and focused more on the positive and put my trust in the Lord, the depression left.

Though it was hard moving into a nursing home some good did come out of it. I am able to reach out to seniors living in the home. Some are put there and forgotten about. A lot of those in a nursing home don't get many or any visitors. I am a volunteer in my nursing home. I get to spend one-on-one time with them and sing to them. I use music therapy with some of the residents. What seemed like a bad thing, turned out for the good because of being able to bring comfort to other residents. Reaching out to others got my focus off my own problems. When Covid hit I had to stop volunteering for awhile because of the restrictions that were put in place.

As I mentioned earlier, I wanted to be a missionary in a foreign country. That hasn't changed, because I can still be a missionary in my own city, reaching out to others. I am a missionary where I live. I've done outreach to the homeless even though I'm in a wheelchair. A lot of times I forget that I'm in a wheelchair. My wheelchair is just a vehicle to get me around. One advantage I have is I don't have to pay for gas.

A lot of times I'm smiling and joking around. People have stopped me and asked me why I'm so happy. They say they see me in a wheelchair driving around all the time and I'm smiling. They want to know the source of my joy. I tell them the reason I can be joyful, even in the midst of the pain, is because of Jesus in my life. He is the source of my joy. I don't know how I would handle what I go through without Him. I don't go around smiling all the time. I have my rough days where I need a good cry. I have a good cry and then move on.

One time, when I still lived on my own, I and another resident of the apartment building I lived in were sitting outside talking. He offered me a beer, but I told him I don't drink beer. He then said, "well you must be on drugs." I told him I wasn't on drugs either. I asked him why he thought I was on drugs. He said because every time he sees me, I'm smiling. He said I must be on something to be that happy. I told him I wasn't on anything, that Jesus is the source of my joy.

One time I and a family member were talking about what age we wanted to live until. I was telling the family member that I wanted to live to be at least ninety years old. They asked me why I would want to live that long with the way I suffer. They said if they were in my shoes they wouldn't want to live that long. I told them that even though I suffer and am in a wheelchair and spend a lot of time in bed because of the disease, I still have a lot to give and that I am very active, even when I'm stuck in bed.

While stuck in bed, I've done music courses online, I've written a book. I write songs and make lyric videos of my songs online. I make candy arrangements and design T-shirts and do some other work, all from bed. The past few years I haven't been able to get out of bed much because it's extremely painful sitting in my wheelchair.

I don't let the disease or being in a wheelchair or even being stuck in bed stop me from being productive. I still live life to the fullest possible with my condition. Since being diagnosed with the disease and being stuck in a wheelchair, I have written over 300 songs. I have recorded a CD called "I want to know You Lord". I have written 54 Biblical word search puzzle books and written a devotional. Presently I am writing an autobiography. I've gone to bible college and taken online courses. I went on a two-week mission trip to Mexico in the early stages of the disease before I was in a wheelchair. I've led worship, done local outreaches, and ministered in many churches.

I've worked or volunteered the whole time I've been in a wheelchair. I was on the planning committee for the March for Jesus in my city for ten years. I have planned several twenty-four-hour worship events in my city. I don't share about these accomplishments to brag about myself, or to say I'm better than anyone else.

It's by the grace of God I've done all these things. I share them as an encouragement for those who are dealing with a disability. Your disability doesn't define you and you can still accomplish things in life. No matter what you're going through, find something you enjoy doing and do it with all your heart. God has given everyone gifts and abilities.

You may not be able to do what I'm able to do but find something you can do and do it with all your heart.

Most importantly, look to God for your strength. He can help you through anything. No matter what you're going through at the moment, remember, things will get better. God is with you to bring the comfort you need.

Author Bio: Tammy Allen

Tammy Allen is a Christian singer/songwriter and author who resides in Windsor, Ontario Canada. Tammy became a Christian when she was 14 years old. Her relationship with God is the most important thing in her life.

Tammy has faced many challenges in her life, including a painful and crippling disease. She has learned to be an overcomer. She doesn't let her disability stop her from accomplishing things in life.

It is her faith in God that has helped her face every challenge she has been through, and to move forward in the midst of each challenge. Tammy has written 54 Biblical word search puzzle books and a devotional book. She is currently writing an inspirational book called "A Song in the Night," which details being an overcomer even in the midst of physical pain and disability. She has written over 300 praise and worship songs, and recorded a CD called "I Want to Know You Lord." She is going to be recording a second CD called "Near to Your Heart."

You can reach Tammy Allen at: inhispresencepublishing@yahoo.com

My Grief Journey

Written by Anne Marie Hartford, M.Ed

I was 43 years old when my father died. I had not had a close encounter with death until then.

We knew two years prior that he had an aneurism on the aorta that would burst at any time. It would be a quick and painless death if something else did not get him before the aneurism ruptured.

It was December 26, 1990 and we had just arrived in Toronto for a visit with my husband's family. The phone call came announcing my dad's death just as we entered my in-laws' apartment. It was out of the question to travel for the funeral which was to take place within 24 hours in the Dominican Republic.

Because I knew that I had little experience dealing with death and grieving, I had started reading self-help books on the subject a few months before he died. I had a very busy life at the time of my father's death. I was married and raising two teenagers, a daughter 15 and a son 17. I also had a full-time job that saw me crisscrossing the province (New Brunswick) on a regular basis. I was typically away from home 2-3 nights per week. My husband also travelled a distance to and from work every day. He was on the road at 6:30 am and not home before 6 pm.

One piece of advice I followed after my dad's death was to actively grieve him rather than trying to ignore, or worst yet, numb the pain with distractions or self-medicating. My father lived in another country and few of my Canadian friends and family had met him. This meant that I was grieving practically alone.

Every Sunday afternoon I would go to my room, close the door, play my dad's favorite music, and look at pictures of my family of origin. I would invariably have a good cry and in a couple of hours I would feel better. I did that on several Sundays.

Less than three months later my husband was killed on his way to work one early Thursday morning.

Looking back, I was glad I had actively grieved my dad even for a few weeks because now I was gripped with a grief that was overwhelming.

We had been living in a small community for almost 10 years by then and the support, help, and outpouring of love was incredibly helpful and valuable to me and my children.

I found it hard to be there for my children, to be of much support to them, when I was devastated. I was glad they had as many friends surrounding them as I had surrounding me.

I engaged many friends and family in making decisions, choosing things like the flowers and organizing the visitations and funeral.

Part of me felt at peace because my husband and I had had many discussions about our time of death. It was part of the Marriage Encounter tradition to encourage participants to talk about deeply meaningful things.

He had told me that he thought he would die young, in a car accident, instantly. His only fear was the car burning. He was 44 years of age when he died, the impact of the head-on collision resulted in immediate death, and the car did not burn. I am eternally grateful to have had those conversations.

Not long after that, my oldest sister died suddenly at the age of 66. I felt like my whole life had shattered. I now felt completely alone in the world. Every one of my main supports had collapsed – and now what?

Like with my father, she lived in the Dominican Republic, and it was not realistic to go for the funeral. Once again, I was grieving alone and while still barely keeping my head above water in the grips of grief for my husband.

My only brother died also at a relatively young age, 69, from lung cancer. Enrique had been smoking three packs of cigarettes a day for close to 60 years - we were not surprised when he was diagnosed. He chose no treatment for which I was very proud of him.

What I have learned is that each death is unique, and the grieving is as unique as the relationship. At times I have not felt much grief for close relatives and yet I have experienced intense grief for some friends.

I had been preparing for my mother's death for so long that when it came, at the age of 94, it was a complete relief. She had spent years in a wheelchair and was miserable.

Regarding the stages of grief this book is based on, I never experienced anger or resentment. It is referred to in literature so persistently that I was concerned that I wasn't feeling it and accessed counselling two years after the death of my husband to make sure I wasn't suppressing or repressing. I was not. What I learned from my experience is that anger and resentment is based on blaming – God, the black ice, the road conditions, etc.

I don't believe in the god of religions so no god to blame. I recognized very quickly that regardless of the unbelievable sense of loss that I needed to choose to accept that life unfolds in perfection, and this includes the good, the bad, and the ugly.

The image I conjured was that of my life being a painting and having that painting ripped in half. Nothing was the same after that day.

I have a sense that I grieved well. I still miss him after more than 30 years, but I have no regrets. I did have other romantic relationships, but none fulfilled me in the way that I had known.

What I say to others is:
Your grief is as unique as your relationship was. Give yourself permission to experience and express thoughts and emotions in safe ways. If you must pay to have someone listen to your crazy-making emotions, don't hesitate. It is, in my opinion, imperative to have at least a few sessions with a grief counsellor to explore what's in your head and heart. It is easier to tell a counsellor who you may never see again about all the crazy experiences and feelings.

Author Bio: Anne Marie Hartford, M.Ed

Born in the Dominican Republic, Anne Marie moved to Canada when she was a teenager not speaking a word of English. Now, having been in Canada for over 50 years, she has not only mastered the English language but also attained a Bachelor's degree in Psychology and Sociology from St. Thomas University and a Master's degree in Adult Education from the University of New Brunswick.

Anne Marie puts action into the ideology of giving back. For the last 20 years, she's been devoted to improving her community through her work managing charitable organizations such as Canadian Mental Health Association, Miramichi Branch and NB Division; Meals on Wheels of Fredericton; and most recently Family Enrichment and Counselling Service.

She's also helped hundreds of people find new and innovative ways of addressing life's challenges, big and small, through her development and facilitation of personal and professional development programs in the areas of psychological wellness and practical life management. As a monthly columnist, Anne Marie has shared her expertise with over eighty published newspaper columns.

Anne Marie has lived in Fredericton, New Brunswick, Canada since 1992. She has two grown children and four grandchildren.

Dinner is at Six

Written by Leona Ottens

Loosing my husband, Matt Ottens, made me feel like I was dead too.

We had 4 kids in 3 years, and they were looking at me to be stable for them.

Matt had survived cancer; he survived an accident with the table saw. He could do anything. Realizing our superman wasn't able to overcome this one hurt so, so, bad.

He was a farmer and partnered with his father. They had a relationship that inspired others.

His last word was my name; "Leona."

June 13th, 2021, I died. June 14th, I realized I'm dead inside, but my organs are still working. Knowing I'd be in the fight of my life to keep myself alive.

One day, sitting by a river with his dad, he noticed the water goes around the island of willows and meets on the other side. He said, "That's how it is. We will meet again when we merge from this side of eternity to the other."

It's Matt! I begged God to switch us. I begged God take me instead. I begged, let me have him and I'll hide him and know one will know he is alive. None of those prayers were answered in the way I wanted them to be.

A rainy cold day in October, in the middle of the field, I cried out, "When will I not be so angry?"

I knew I needed to go back to the lake. Go back to the water. Baptism.

No! That's too hard, that's asking too much! I could not deny the peace I felt thinking of it.

I had been baptised as a seven-year-old, but it didn't mean anything to me, and I was afraid. I was trying to surrender to God, but I couldn't let go of the pain.

I felt peace thinking of coming out of that water with the breath my husband fought so hard for and taking it and living what is left of this life to the fullest. And so, eight months later, at the one-year mark, I was baptised.

Our families and loved ones wrapped around us. A pastor who was a very important part of my healing baptized me. Under the same sky. In Matt's doorway. We all have a doorway. Some on the side of the road. Some in the comfort of their bed. Matt's was a lake. A beautiful blue sky above and he went through it and into heaven. I surrendered all the pain to God. I knew I was not alone.

One of my kids said to me, "You made it safe again, Mom."

The next day my kids went in the water again.

If the devil can convince us, (or if not religious) if we convince ourselves that we are alone, we will not fulfill our purpose or experience real joy. Alone on a manure pad I laid. In the muddy field. On the bathroom floor. Knowing...I am not alone. When it says in the Bible...

Psalm 34:18 *He is close to the broken hearted.* (NLT)

I understand why people consider suicide. I did. But I couldn't because I had the kids to think about.

He shields us from being there alone. Because if we are convinced, we are alone, we become selfish and stuck in a lonely, victimized place.

Somewhere someone else is suffering bad in the same way and different ways.

Somewhere someone is stuck and paralyzed by grief and somewhere else someone has overcome it.

All those people are in it with us together.

We are not alone. It's selfish to think we are. It is normal to feel grief, but not forever!

We need to love each other while it is our turn.

That's what we can do.

When our loved one comes home, and we get to go to them it's our turn, so we get to be present in it.

I'm so grateful for love. For family.

Getting groceries and crying in front of his favorite ice cream, realizing someone else somewhere can't breathe in the diaper isle because it was a size 4 diaper they didn't get to buy for their baby. Realizing newborn diapers was the last purchase someone made, and they would not be used. The French's ketchup staple or hot sauce. Oh my... all these products... all those people.
We are not alone.

It will be okay. Even when we don't think it.

Matt survived cancer 5 years before the accident.

We had to have hard conversations about what if? One day finding out he has cancer and the next day finding out I was expecting twins. That's life. A roller coaster. We made rules for if worst came to worst.

Dinner is at six.

You don't need to do anything but breathe but dinner is at six. I peeled myself from whatever laying position I was paralyzed in and sometimes could only stomach water or smoothies, but I was at the table with my kids at six.

Do not loose faith.
That's weak. And it's weak to only have faith when things are good.

Do not drink alone.
The kids need you and when you have a drink it will be to Celebrate. Bottles of wine given to us went down the drain. Then I filled them with water, and I chugged them. I couldn't keep them in the house because I didn't trust myself.

Keep your heart open and if you get the chance, love again.

Take care of each other's family.

Never lose your sense of humor.

Matt liked a good laugh. He didn't want us to feel guilty for laughing. Laughter is a good thing.

Keep your health.

My exercise routine saved me.

I had gotten myself into routine for the kids' sake.

I was blessed with a space in the bank barn designed by my husband before he died. The foundation was poured. He passed away the day before they started building.

He didn't know it, but that room saved me.

What a gift.

Being a personal trainer for years and not being able to get to work. I stumbled down to the barn and taught neighbors how to move and groove. We cried and we prayed.

Consistency has led to me having a bounce in my step. It encouraged me to sleep knowing I had to get up. The kids joined skating and were doing as well as they could in school. They could eat and sleep and we could laugh together. Inside I was so dead. So sad. So broken. That's why I cried out in the field.

These rules have gotten us this far. God is good and we have been able to turn our anger about a lot of things into gratitude. Even waiting for him to come out of the lake for six hours. Some never find their loved ones. For some the search goes on for weeks. I got to lay on him. I got to kiss him. I got vomit in my hair that I didn't want to wash off because it was his. I sat in our bed holding my crying kids and when they exhausted themselves and fell asleep, I washed it off and I knew dinner was at six.

Everyone has something going on or they will have. All we can do is give it to God and keep living and loving.

So many people are grieving. Let joy pull you through.

Give it to God because it is too much to carry.

Matt Ottens has inspired me to live a life fully with all my heart as he did. He was there for his family and friends with a laugh I'll always know. I got to experience an incredible marriage.

No regrets. No fear. Matt wasn't afraid to die. He LOVED like crazy every day. His family and his friends can still hear his laugh.

It will be okay.

We are not victims of our circumstances. We aren't heroes. We are regular people who are all in this thing called life together.

Let's love one another.

Dinner is at six.

Keep your heart open.

Author Bio: Leona Ottens

Leona lives in southern Ontario, Canada. Mama to four kids, ages 10, 8, 7 and 7. Four wild kiddos born in three years. Through her twin pregnancy her husband fought cancer and she grew very large.

She is a farmer and personal trainer since she was 17. They share their farm with the community to stay fit for regular workouts and euchre nights.

They host the Shine Your Light Sunflower Tour each year. The community gathers to listen to live music, shop in a market with local vendors and take a walk through the sunflower field reading comical and uplifting signs.

They also host a run or walk to raise money for the local hospital. The first year was to celebrate Matt's five-years in remission. The second was to have a celebration of life for him because of Covid restrictions they couldn't honor him the way he deserved so they found a way. The third was to continue to live. And the fourth is coming up this August. So far, the community has raised over $50,000.

Leona enjoys sports of any kind for fun. She holds a Guineas World Record for most burpees done by a team in 12 hours.

She gets to compete at OWA weightlifting competitions in Ontario and it's amazing to see what people are capable of. It's helped a lot during grief and before it.

They are blessed to live 1Km from her folks and across the road from her in-laws. They farm together. It is so hard without Matt but they lean on each other. She is thankful her husband taught her years ago how to drive equipment because she can keep doing it now.

Leona enjoys singing in church. She gets to be on the Terry Fox committee with a bunch of great people. It's wonderful to come together and honor Terry each year.

She is learning to play guitar. Leona enjoys road trips with her kids. They hit the road and if they don't have what they need they make do with something. They enjoy sitting on top of the van and taking in the views. Sharing meals up there and getting away from the stink they created in the van.

Coaching her kids' soccer team and playing catch with them means so much to Leona. To get to know them and to love them as much as she gets to before her doorway opens.

Leona ends with, "I'm a regular girl with big dreams of experiencing this life to the fullest with the ones I love."

Then Jesus Came

Written by Tammy Leigh Robinson

I've had a few tragedies in my life which have caused me grief. None of them came close to the day my daughter Wendy died. She was 6 months and 11 days old. Wendy was a content and happy baby. She slept through the night when she was only 1 1/2 months old!

When Christmas came, she was only two months old, so she slept a lot and I only took two pictures. I never dreamed that would be her only Christmas with us. I remember thinking, *I'll take more pictures next Christmas.*

In her sixth month, when I took her for a check up, I told our family doctor that it sounded like she was wheezing. I've had asthma since I was a kid so I'm familiar with the sound. After the doctor listened to her chest, he said she wasn't wheezing and that sometimes when there is mucus in the throat it can sound like it's wheezing in her chest.

I agreed that right at that moment she wasn't wheezing, but I was adamant that she had been wheezing the previous night. Then I explained that she always seemed to have a head cold. She'd go on anti-biotics and would be better for a few weeks and then it came back. I asked if maybe we should send her to a specialist.

Our family doctor said other than the recurring head colds she was healthy. Her weight was right in line with where she should be for a six-month-old. He suggested we wait another month and see how she was at that time, after this new round of anti-biotics.

That was Wednesday.

Saturday night my husband Bill, and I went on a date night. When we came home the babysitter told us Wendy wasn't feeling well. It seemed like she was struggling to breathe.

Every night before I went to bed, I would place my hand on my children's backs and pray for them. On this night, when I prayed for Wendy, I had an odd thought that this was the last time I was going to do this. I shook off the feeling and chalked it up to I was just worrying over nothing. After all, the doctor said she's healthy.

Wendy didn't sleep well that night and by 5 am I had brought her into our bed so she could be with us. We didn't have a car at the time, so at 6 am I called my parents and asked them to give us a ride to the hospital and to look after my two-year-old son.

While I was getting dressed, I looked at Wendy -our baby -lying in the middle of our bed. She looked so cute and comfy. Another foreboding thought came to my mind that this will be the last time I see her in our bed. Again, I shook it off and chalked it up to being a worried mommy.

We were in the Emergency Room for several hours. They admitted her to the hospital and put her in a tent with oxygen. Finally, our family doctor came in and talked to us. He said, "Remember when you came to see me on Wednesday, you said you wanted her to see a specialist? Well, we're going to send her to the Orillia hospital so the paediatrician can see what she's like when she's sick."

We took him at his word. We later discovered the truth was she was really sick and he couldn't help her. She NEEDED to see a specialist!

As I mentioned we didn't have a vehicle. I was permitted to ride in the ambulance with Wendy, while my husband contacted friends to borrow their truck to drive to Orillia, Ontario, which was about an hour away from our home.

When we first arrived at the Orillia hospital, we were in the Emergency Department. I was surprised to see a friend from school whose name is Wendy. She was one of the people I had in mind when we named our daughter Wendy.

You see, we believe a person's name is very important and we considered people we knew with that name and asked ourselves, do we want our children to turn out like that person.

My friend Wendy was more of an acquaintance than a close friend. We'd spent some time together outside school, but not much. However, I knew her to be someone who was kind, gentle and loving. I had lost touch with her after school, and it was a surprise and a comfort to have her working on my baby girl, her namesake.

After awhile, Wendy was settled upstairs in her own room. The nurses asked me a lot of questions. I also didn't realize that she was in the Intensive Care Unit. I thought she was in a regular room. I sat by her side, praying fervently that God would heal her.

Later, when Bill arrived, we decided to make arrangements to stay in Orillia overnight. We had friends who lived there, and we wanted to ask if we could stay with them. By this time, it was nearing supper hour. Neither of us had eaten all day, and Wendy seemed to be sleeping peacefully. We told the nurses we were going to get something to eat.

Again, there was a lack of communication.

We meant we were leaving the hospital to get food and make arrangements with our friends to spend the night. The nursing staff thought we were going to get food from the cafeteria.

We went to Arby's and ate a quick dinner. Then we stopped in for a brief visit to ask our friends about staying the night with them. They said of course we could stay there. As soon as that was taken care of, I asked to use her phone (this was before the days of cell phones) to call the hospital to check on Wendy.

When I was put through to the nurse, I could hear stress in her voice. She said the doctor needed to speak with us and asked what number he could reach us at. I asked my friend what her number was. I was confused because we hadn't even seen the doctor before we left the hospital. The nurse's voice was filled with urgency when she said, "The doctor NEEDS to speak to you!"

I hung up the phone and walked into the next room to join Bill and our friend, telling them about the conversation with the nurse.

I didn't even sit down before the phone rang. We knew it was the doctor, so I answered it. I was shocked by his words. Wendy had gone into cardiac arrest and was on life support. I couldn't believe it! We had left her less than 30 minutes ago and she was sleeping peacefully!

While trying to take in the doctor's words I motioned to my husband that he needed to pick up the extension phone so he could hear what the doctor was saying. The doctor went on to say Wendy may not live and if she did live, she would be a vegetable, not able to move or talk because she had gone so long without oxygen, he expected her brain would have been damaged.

We immediately left our friends' house and raced to the hospital. Outside her room a nurse met us and tried to prepare us for what we were about to see. Nothing she said could have prepared me for that shock. The ventilation tube was in her mouth, and she had wires hooked up to her chest, head, and extremities. It was hard to see my baby through all the wires and tubes. I later found out the wires were monitoring her saturation of oxygen levels as well as monitoring her heart and lungs.

It was later explained to us that she had acute bronchiolitis. Bronchitis is when the large vessels of the lungs fill with mucus. Bronchiolitis is when the mucus has progressed to plug the small bronchioles of her lungs. Oxygen wasn't getting through to her organs or her extremities.

As broken as I was, I stepped beside my daughter's bedside and laid my hand gently on her chest. I prayed over her asking God for a miraculous healing. I even prayed in tongues (a gift of the Holy Spirit).

Suddenly, alarms started going off. The doctor and nurses asked us to step back.

As we stood at the end of her bed watching without really seeing them work on her, Wendy opened her eyes and looked at us. She gave us a big, beautiful smile!

That smile was one of the greatest blessings from God in that dark, difficult time. She knew Mommy and Daddy were there with her and she was telling us not to worry. Jesus was taking care of her.

A nurse took us to a quiet room where we could sit and pray. We didn't realize at the time, but the alarms were signalling that she had gone into cardiac arrest again. The doctor needed to resuscitate her. After a few minutes a nurse came in and told us, "She's back with us, but keep praying."

We were so relieved! We used a payphone to call both of our parents. We told them, "Wendy is really sick, and she might die!" Both parents got in their vehicles for the one-hour trip to Orillia.

A lot happened within that hour. Wendy, the nurse from ED came upstairs and joined us in prayer. Our friends whose house we were going to stay at also came and joined us in the room to pray. Several times we heard the announcement over the PA system that called Code Blue Stat.

A nurse would come in and tell us her heart had failed again and the doctor is working on her. We'd cry and pray even harder. Later the

51

nurse would return to tell us she's back with us. This happened so many times I lost track. The night seemed so long. We had lost all sense of time.

Finally, after the nurse had told us the doctor was working on her again, I realized it had been a very long time since she'd told us that. Several minutes had gone by. I knew it would take a miracle to resuscitate her again.

Suddenly, my mind went to a book series I had read a few times. The series is called Love Comes Softly, and it was written by Janette Oak. It is a Christian romance pioneer series. The part that came to my mind was when the dad had an accident, and his leg was infected with gangrene. There was no doctor, and they were doing the best they could to save his life. His grown daughter Missy and her Mama were praying together for a miracle to heal him and spare his life. When the Mama prayed, she asked for God's will to be done.

Missy became angry with her mama, saying, to pray for Papa's healing even if it wasn't God's will. Her mama reminded her that her Papa always wanted God's will in his life. If it was his time to go, then they needed to release him to God. He wouldn't be happy if God spared his life when it wasn't God's will.

This was very hard for Missy to accept but she did eventually accept it and joined her mama in praying for God's will even if it meant her Papa dying.

I heard the still, small, peaceful voice of my Saviour saying, "It is time to give Wendy back to me." I struggled with that in silent prayer. "God, she's, MY baby! I love her so much!"

I remembered in the book; the father had his leg amputated and lived. Did God need us to relinquish our hold on Wendy as a test? Was He testing us to see if we loved Him more than our daughter? Would He miraculously heal her if we gave her to Him? I realized God knows our hearts and He would know if we were trying to trick Him by saying we give her to God but really meaning, so you can heal her and bring her back to us.

Then I remembered something I had said to my husband, while holding Wendy, exactly one week prior. We had just come home from church. We were talking about our friends who had shared a testimony that they had found their daughter floating in the pool. They got her out and performed CPR on her. She came back to life and is healthy again. The words I had said to my husband were, "I could never handle it if one of our kids died!"

I realized in that moment that the scripture verse in Philippians 4:13 (NLT), "I can do everything through Christ who gives me strength," was either true or not. My faith was tested. Did I truly believe God's Word? Would Jesus really give me strength to endure the tragic death of my daughter?

At that moment I realized I did believe. I had faith. In that moment I was flooded with peace. I could feel God's loving arms around me in that little room filled with prayers. I silently prayed, "Okay Lord... she's yours to take home to heaven or to miraculously heal. I have faith in You that Your will is what is the very best."

Filled with peace I heard God's still small voice again. "Share that with Bill." I lifted my head, took a deep breath, and looked across the room at my husband. He was sitting on a chair in the corner. His head was bowed in prayer. His face was contorted in anguish.

I am the type of person who talks about the books I read to the people around me. The characters in the books become almost real to me, especially when it is a book series. So, when I started talking to Bill about Missy and her mama praying, he remembered me telling him about that when I had read it. Then I said, "We need to give Wendy back to God."

I remember him shaking his head, then bowing in prayer again. I knew he was wrestling with God. The Holy Spirit whispered to me, "Pray for him." So, in that moment my prayers changed. I started praying for the man I loved to hear God speak to him and to know beyond a shadow of a doubt that God will give us the strength to go through whatever our path ahead may be.

Again, as I prayed, I realized Wendy had been "down" for a long time. I knew in my heart that she was dying. My eyes were on Bill as I prayed for him. Finally, he raised his head and looked me in the eye. He gave a sad, slight nod to me. In that small act I knew that he had given our daughter back to her Heavenly Father.

The most amazing part of this story to me, is that it was only SECONDS later when the doctor walked in. As soon as I saw him, I knew Wendy had died. In my anguish I realized God had not taken her until both Bill and I had relinquished her to him.

Our Father is a gentleman. Not everyone gets to experience this. For some reason God knew that we needed the opportunity to come to terms with Wendy's mortality BEFORE she died.

It's been almost 34 years since that Sunday night. I'm sure some of my memories have faded but many of them are as clear as the day it happened.

I remember going back to Wendy's room and holding her dead body in my arms. She was my baby. She was so heavy and lifeless. It was agonizing and yet I didn't want to let go of her. How could I? I knew this was the last time I'd ever hold her, so I wanted it to last as long as possible.

Suddenly, the door burst open, and my parents rushed into the room. My mom's face was distorted with anguish as she cried out, "Is she okay?"

The hardest thing I had to do was look up at my mom and say, "She died Mom!"

I later found out that the staff thought my parents already knew she had died.

They didn't realize that they had been driving for over an hour. So, when my in-laws arrived the staff gently gave them the news of Wendy's death before admitting them into her room. I remember our pastors also arrived and prayed with us.

Finally, the time came that I had to physically release my baby. As the tears flowed down my face and dropped off my chin, I felt anguish and peace at the same time.

My heart felt like it was torn out, yet I knew Wendy was in the arms of Jesus at that moment. I knew with every fiber of my being that she was happy and healthy and that no harm would ever come to her. She was in the very best place she could be.

The nurses asked us if we wanted to go to the Chapel. I know they needed us to get going so they could take care of Wendy's body, but I just wasn't ready to leave.

As we walked down the hall, the tears still flowing freely, I remember passing people in the hall.

I remember thinking, "How can they be happy? My world has been obliterated!" I also remember feeling like they should be able to see by looking at me that my baby girl had just died, as if I had a sign on me that read, "Grieving Mother". Even at the time I knew my thoughts, weren't making sense.

Mom and Dad drove us to their house that night. I remember feeling so empty as I realized I had left my baby girl in Orillia, and I was going home without her.

One of our friends from church had a baby girl who had died the year before. One of my parents gave them a call and even though it was past midnight she came over. I remember her wrapping her loving arms around me and I bawled on her shoulder. There was a measure of comfort knowing that she knew my pain. I don't remember her saying anything. Words weren't needed. I just needed the loving act of holding me and letting me cry.

That night I lay in bed, not able to sleep, trying to think through the fog of shock and grief. At some point I drifted off to sleep. When I woke, I remembered dreaming about Wendy rolling down a grassy knoll, laughing and giggling.

I realized God had blessed me once again. Over the next little while I remembered the different times God had tried to prepare me for Wendy's death, like when I prayed over her that last night and when she was laying in our bed. I was grateful to know that God was caring for us through the whole situation.

A couple days later, just the day before Wendy's funeral, I remember sitting at Mom and Dad's table. Many people came and went, giving us their condolences. I was brewing with anger as people kept saying, "I know it hurts."

I know people were trying to help, but it angered me because they DIDN'T KNOW! It's different if your grandma or your uncle dies after living a full life. It is not natural for a parent to bury their child. The parents are supposed to die before the children. As I sat there stewing inwardly, my parents' neighbour walked in. She didn't say a word. She just came and put her arms around me.

You see, her son, a school mate of mine, had died the summer before. She DID KNOW the pain of losing her child. The comfort her hug brought me cannot be put into words.

During her funeral our pastor read a poem he'd written called, "Then Jesus Came." It was a huge comfort to me. Unfortunately, there is no record of the poem. Essentially, there was a statement; then Jesus came. Another statement. Then Jesus came. Another statement. Then Jesus came. And so on. Each time when Jesus came, He brought help, healing and comfort.

The days that followed were like a fog. I remember as the cars left the graveyard, the man who lived across the road from the graveyard was directing traffic. It was such a simple act, but it gave me a bit of comfort.

We had been staying at Mom and Dad's house until after the funeral. Some ladies from the church went into our home and removed the crib, change table and other things that would be a painful reminder of our loss. I appreciated that they left her pretty, white dresser so when I was ready, I could go through her clothes.

I don't know when I finally got around to doing it, but I do remember holding one of her hats. There were a few of her hairs inside the hat. I gathered the hairs in my fingers and cried. I missed her so much!

I felt so empty. Until then, whenever I left the house, I had a baby in one arm, diaper bag and purse slung over my shoulder and was holding my son's hand with my other arm. Suddenly my arms were empty. Yes, I had my son, and I was glad for that. When I had thoughts that I didn't want to live without Wendy I remembered that I had my son to take care of. He needed me. I grew strong because I had to be strong for him. Poor Steven was only two years old. He didn't understand why his sister wasn't here anymore.

Several times I remember standing at the kitchen sink doing dishes and feeling empty and alone. "God," I said, out loud, "I really need a hug!" I literally felt loving arms wrapped around me in a hug. I knew our friends and family were praying for us. I could feel it. I don't know how to describe it, but I could feel it. I felt both weak and strong at the same time. I felt both devastation and joy at the same time. I felt grateful and angry at the same time.

Though I didn't feel angry at God when Wendy died, there was a time later that summer when I was furious with God. A dear sweet lady in our church died after Wendy did. A co-worker of my husband and my Dad's also died. Then another co-worker committed suicide, killing her little girl with her.

It was the "straw that broke the camel's back". All these deaths were piling grief upon grief, and I felt like I couldn't take anymore. I screamed at God. Bill held me as I pounded my fists on his chest, crying, "Why God? Why are you taking so many people away from us?"

I remember a day when I was in the drugstore, and I made a scene. I don't remember what it was that went wrong, and I know I wasn't angry over that little thing. Looking back, I realized my grief needed expression and it just came out that day.

Weeks after Wendy died, I was struggling with depression. I was trying to be a good mom to Steven, and I was also very broken. I'm eternally grateful that I had a strong faith in God because He gave me the strength I needed.

One day my parents dropped in for a visit. I remember standing in my dark living room and Mom had her arms wrapped around me as I cried on her shoulder. After awhile, Dad interrupted my sobbing with, "You need to pull yourself together. Think about your son. Wendy died, you didn't. You have to get on with your life. Open up your curtains to let the sunshine in. Put on some worship music and pull yourself out of this funk."

Those are probably not his exact words, but that was the gist of it. Then he went out the door. I burst into a fresh stream of tears. *How could he talk to me that way? Didn't he know my baby girl is dead?*

Mom held me for a few minutes and crooned to me that, "Your dad loves you. He can't stand to see you like this. He's trying to help you."

Dad was honking the horn, so mom gave me a squeeze and walked out the door. I collapsed on the sofa and bawled like a baby for a long time. Eventually, Dad's words broke through the fog of grief and made their way into my heart. They were followed by Mom's assurances that Dad loves me and was trying to help.

Finally, I stood up and opened the curtains. I put on some worship music. I stood in my living room and raised my hands in worship. I didn't FEEL like doing any of that, but I knew in my heart and my head that Dad and Mom were right. At first, I just stood there letting the gentle music wash over me, healing my broken heart. Eventually, I found my voice and I started to sing along with the music.

That difficult experience was a turning point in my grief. Oh yes, I still had bad days but as each day passed, I grew stronger and stronger.

As you can tell by what I've shared one stage of grief that was very hard for me was depression and loneliness. Eventually, I grew stronger and worked through those dark lonely days.

In the days that followed Wendy's death I felt guilt as well. I was a young mom. Did I do something wrong? Did I cause my daughter's death? Could I have done something different? Bill and I shouldn't have gone out on a date that Saturday night.

I should have taken her to the Emergency Department sooner. I should have demanded my family doctor send her to the specialist. We shouldn't have left the hospital to get dinner. I should have known she was really sick. She basically died while we were out eating dinner! What kind of mother was I?

One day I got a card in the mail. There was a letter with the card as well as a little booklet called Good Grief by Granger E. Westberg. The letter was from a lady I've never met. She heard about my daughter's death. She shared her story with me of her young son dying. Her words of the physical ache she felt for her son resonated with me. I was comforted that even though every situation is different, there are other people who know pain like mine.

The book, Good Grief talks about the 10 stages of grief. It was a valuable resource to me. I realized that it is normal to go through stages more than once and sometimes even more than one stage at a time. It is normal to feel grief like waves of the ocean. Sometimes they push you around, but your feet stay firmly planted on bottom. Other times the waves knock you off your feet, even to the point of holding you under water until you feel you cannot breathe, and you think you will drown in the heaviness of it.

It is because of this woman, whom I still don't know, that I have compiled this book, Stories of Good Grief. I realize that the greatest comfort I experienced, other than prayers, was from other mothers who had also lost their child.

My purpose in publishing this book is to bring comfort to people who are grieving, whether it's due to the death of a loved one, or the loss of your health or the loss of a relationship, or anything else that is important to you.

Someone once said, "The emotions we bury are still alive, therefore they will fight and claw to get back out again."

Another person said, "There is no way around a negative emotion. The only way around is through which means we have to process them."

I recently read a book entitled, A Rip In Heaven by Jeanine Cummins. There is a line near the end of the book that grabbed my attention. The character had just released all the guilt he'd felt over his cousins' deaths. "...And in place of all those demons, the small shoots of a pure grief, not laced with rage or distorted by fear. He was finally free to just miss his cousins without any other baggage disrupting that."

If I could travel back in time and say something to myself while I was grieving, I would tell myself to pay more attention to my son. In dealing with my grief, I didn't see that he was grieving as well. I knew he missed Wendy, but I didn't know that as an adult he would still be affected by that loss. I thought because he was so young, he couldn't understand grief. It turns out whether he understood it or not he felt it.

To you who are reading this today, I would encourage you that although time itself doesn't heal your grief, as time passes the pain does get easier to manage. Allow yourself to grieve so you can heal. When we stuff our grief deep down inside ourselves without allowing it to manifest it will fester into bitterness.

The day before Wendy died, I read a devotional for that day, entitled, "Where Is God When Tragedy Strikes?" It is from a book titled Today Can Be Different by Harold J Sala. The final paragraph sums it up so well I want to share it with you...

"Tragedy never leaves us where it finds us; it will either drive us closer towards God or else from His presence. It all depends on where you put the tragedy –between you and God, or behind you. God is not silent in times of tragedy. He speaks through it to the man or woman who listens for His voice."

I hope and pray this book will help you to process the feelings and emotions that come with grief. Remember, you are not alone.

You can do it!

Author Bio: Tammy Leigh Robinson

Tammy Robinson, author of the NAMELESS Trilogy, enjoys bringing the stories in the Bible to life by researching deep into the Jewish culture.

Although Tammy has faced many difficulties in her life, she continues to be goal-oriented and works hard to reach her goals. Known for her optimism and joy, Tammy focuses on helping others, encouraging them to reach their goals and create WIN/ WIN opportunities.

Tammy lives in picturesque Nackawic, New Brunswick with her husband Keith. Tammy and Keith open their home to international students each school year as part of their effort to impact the world. Two of Tammy's grown children live with their families in Ontario and one in Nova Scotia. Her granddaughter and great grandson live in Ontario. Her stepson lives in Fredericton, NB.

My Story

Written By Ralph LeBlanc

The dictionary describes grief as a strong, sometimes overwhelming experience, the result of any of a number of causes.

Personally, I didn't know what grief was until I was 17 and in the army. It was that summer that I learned of the death of my maternal grandfather. He and I were quite close. I often thought of him more as a father than my real father.

A few years later we lost our maternal grandmother whom I loved dearly. I was more grieved for my mother's loss than for my own.

When I lost my father, I was very sad. At the same time, I was happy. He was not a good father, or husband. Shortly before he passed, I had the opportunity to lead him to the Lord. That took a lot of the pain of losing him away.

Mom died soon after. That was a whole new type of grief. However, it was a relief because she had suffered so much in her short life!!!

When my wife, Laverne's dad died, she was so pleased to see how many of her friends shared in her grief and helped her through it. Again, it was sort of a blessing to know that her dad was no longer in pain. I don't mention my paternal family because I never met them.

A few years later I met with a new type of grief, the loss of a sibling. First Laverne lost her oldest brother to cancer. We watched as her mother suffered the loss of a child. That was pain beyond the spoken word. Not long after that, I lost my baby sister to the same killer - cancer. Next it was my mother-in-law, mom Chestnut, but she died just the way she wanted to... in her sleep and at peace with the Lord.

My other sister was next to pass. Again, it was by that dreaded killer, cancer. Yes, we had experienced death and with it a lot of grief, uncles, aunts, cousins, a nephew, other siblings, and dear friends. Many of whom I was called upon to eulogise, but nothing, absolutely nothing could prepare us for the loss of our own dear daughter Susanne.

Just 51 and in her prime, she was loved and admired by all who knew her. She was a great teacher, mother, daughter, sister, wife, and friend. Tell me, how do you get over that kind of loss?

However, again I drew comfort from the fact that she prepared for it years before. When her daughter Erin was born, Susanne made sure that we were well bonded with her daughter by bringing her to us at least once a month over the years, to spend time with us.

Our home became her home, as it always was Susanne's home. How did we deal with our grief? One day at a time. Did we get over it? NO! And we expect we never will. Shortly after she passed, we were asked how we were doing. Our answer was we were down to crying once a day. Their reply was, "Oh, that's great!"

We then went on to say, "Once a day all day long."

Again, I drew comfort from the WORD of God. Quite awhile before her passing I came across a scripture verse that fit Susanne to the letter. Micha 6:8 tells us what God wants from us. To paraphrase it, I read it this way... live justly, love tenderly, and walk humbly. We would all like to do that, but our daughter lived that verse. Without knowing it, she had come across the same thought. It is now written on her tombstone.

Do we still grieve? Yes, and we will until the day we die. But we draw comfort from God's Word and the spirit of our daughter that lives on in her daughter, our grand daughter, Erin. She is 18 years old now and studying to become a civil engineer. She still spends as much time with us as she possibly can, and we appreciate her so much.

Author Bio: Ralph LeBlanc

Ralph was born in Sussex, New Brunswick on December 17th, 1942 to a 21 year-old country girl and a 26 year old spoiled soldier. Both were Acadian French born in NB, though neither spoke French at home. His mom didn't speak French because she didn't know the language. His dad didn't speak it because his French was Acadian.

They moved to Montreal when Ralph was about six years old. Ralph speaks Quebec French. He had three siblings. His two younger sisters died of cancer several years ago. He has a younger brother who lives in Ontario. They are more than brothers –they are very good friends.

Ralph joined the army at 17. In the Royal Canadian Army Service Corp, he went to the Middle East at 19 (1962-1963). When he returned, he met and married Laverne, his wife of 58 years. His son Joe was born in Quebec City in 1965 where he was stationed at the time.

From there he was sent to Germany for three years with NATO (1965-1968). Laverne was pregnant when he left there to return to Canada in August 1968. His daughter Susanne was born in Fredericton in March 1969. He was stationed at CFB Gagetown where he took his release in 1970.

Ralph and Laverne moved to Nackawic in 1974, where Ralph was the department store manager (Walkers). Fire destroyed the shopping center in 1976. Then Ralph went into commercial sales and travelled the Atlantic region for several years until he retired in 2006.

Ralph and his wife were members of the Nackawic Baptist Church for 30 years (1974-2004). Since then, they have attended the Nackawic Wesleyan Church where they still attend. In his 60's Ralph attended lay pastor training and graduated as a lay pastor (Atlantic Baptist Convention of Churches). He chose not to be ordained, preferring rather to take services when other pastors were absent or on vacation.

Ralph and his wife Laverne lost their daughter Susanne to cancer in 2020. They miss her greatly and mourn her loss every day.

My Beautiful Daughter

Written By Laverne LeBlanc

This is a very difficult subject to write about, especially considering that grief touches most of our lives at one time or another.

Our daughter was 50 when she was diagnosed with Stage 1 breast cancer. She had already had two miracles in her life. When she was in her early twenties, she was diagnosed with Stage 1 cervical cancer.

She had surgery, but the doctors didn't think she would ever have children. That was grief in itself for her. She grieved for the children she would never have.

When she was 35, she got pregnant with her daughter, Erin. She called the pregnancy her miracle from God. After 15 years of marriage, they finally had a beautiful baby girl. Our family was so grateful for that precious bundle of joy.

A few months later, the cancer came back, and she had a hysterectomy, but she was satisfied that God had allowed her to have a child.

We're thankful that the first year after the baby was born, she and the baby would come to our house for one week each month. She was determined that we would be very closely bonded with our granddaughter, just in case the cancer came back, and we would be needed to help care for her.

I never gave it much thought because we always loved having our daughter with us. But I think, somehow, she knew that the day would come when mom and dad would have to help fill the void of her loss.

When she first was diagnosed with breast cancer, Stage 1, at the age of 50, everything looked like she would be fine. She decided on a double mastectomy and had chemo and radiation. It was a very long grueling year for all of us, but especially for her. At first the doctors thought the cancer was gone and at that she was preparing to return to teaching at Oromocto High School.

Then, suddenly, she was having problems with falling and forgetting things. After calling the hospital and immediately getting in for an MRI it was discovered that the cancer had metastasized, and she was now in Stage 4 breast cancer.

Susanne was always a very positive person and when we told her we were praying for a miracle, she said God had already given her two miracles: having her daughter and recovering from her first cancer. That was all she would get. She accepted her fate and stated she would not recover this time and that was fine.

Our lives were devastated. We could not imagine living without our beautiful daughter. She was the child that was always there for us, and we had so many wonderful memories of our times together. When I had time alone, I fell to the floor and prayed that God would be merciful and heal Susanne. I could not imagine living without her. Apart from my husband, she was my best friend and confidant; the one I shared everything with.

Now she would be gone forever, and there would be a giant hole in my heart and in my life. As we went through the process of watching her slip away from us, God showed us great mercy. Every day a scripture verse would come to mind or be pointed out to us. We knew that we had to be very strong for her husband and her 15-year-old daughter, so we drew on all the strength that God allowed us to have.

In the end, her first instinct that she would need her parents' help was called to mind. Our granddaughter, Erin has had an especially difficult time and I believe that she lost at least two years of her young life in mourning her mom. She went through anger, and sadness at the loss. How could someone so good and loving be taken, when there were so many bad people in the world?

Erin was 15 when her mom died, which is a difficult time in a young person's life at the best of times. She spends most holidays with us and as soon as university classes are finished on Fridays, she drives to our place for the weekend.

God may take, but He also gives in return. I thank Him every day for our granddaughter. She cannot take her mom's place, but she fills a void in our lives.

One thing that helped me during that time was reading a book called Being with Dying by Joan Halifax. This book encouraged me during those difficult days at the end of her life. I recommend reading this book if you or someone you love is in the process of dying.

After our daughter passed away, some of our friends that had lost their children came by with words of encouragement. We could understand their loss just by the look of pain on their faces. They helped us cope with each day. Although my husband and I had each lost parents and siblings, we had no idea how overwhelming losing our child could possibly be.

The pain and grief stayed with us for many days and months. At first, I thought we just had to get through this period, but then we realized that one does not ever get through it. We must learn to deal with our loss.

One scripture that was of great comfort was Psalm 56:8, "You keep track of all my sorrows.   You have collected all my tears in your

your bottle. You have recorded each one in your book." (NLT) God knows all our heartaches and He will give us His strength to cope with each day.

Author Bio: Laverne LeBlanc

Laverne lives in Nackawic, New Brunswick. She had two children, Joe LeBlanc and Susanne (LeBlanc) McKay. Her children were fortunate to grow up in this unique, small town of Nackawic. Laverne worked at the Nackawic High School for 31 years as Administrative Assistant. She felt very fortunate to be able to watch her children go through school and be handy to them at all times.

Laverne and her husband Ralph have always attended church. At first it was the United Baptist Church and later the Nackawic Wesleyan Church. All through her children's growing up years, Ralph and Laverne worked with Sunday School and Young People's groups.

Laverne worked with Red Cross, Nackawic Wellness Committee and is presently part of the Comfort Quilters Women's group. They quilt for people with cancer and other serious illnesses. This is one of the most fulfilling volunteer positions she has had the privilege to belong to.

Laverne's daughter died in 2020 of breast cancer. Now their lives have significantly changed. They have their granddaughter at their home most weekends and days when she is off university. Even after her great loss, Laverne says God has blessed them in many ways.

My Strong Right Arm

Written by Heather Knight Ashby

I am the oldest of two children. My brother, Michael, was two-and-a-half years younger than me. Growing up we didn't have a lot of "extras". We had our basic necessities and not much more. What we did have in abundance was laughter. Michael and I were born in the late '60's and growing up in that era it was the general rule that the older child was responsible for the younger one(s).

There wasn't much Michael got into trouble for, but it didn't seem to bother me much. Michael was the best gift my parents ever gave me! We shared a lot of laughs in our short time together. We got into a lot of mischief together as well.

When Michael was in about Grade four, one day on the school playground at recess he broke his arm. It was such a bad break that it required surgery to repair. That meant blood work was needed. This is where our lives started to turn upside down. His blood cell count came back, and the numbers were way off from where they should have been.

Over the course of the next four years, Michael had many trips to the doctor's office and several to Sick Kids Hospital (S.K.) in Toronto. On one of those visits at S.K. doctors were finally able to tell my parents what was actually wrong with him; Michael needed a liver transplant.

In April 1984, at London University Hospital (L.U.H.) in London, Ontario Michael had his transplant surgery. In July of that same year, we celebrated his 15th birthday with a renewed sense of hope. As he blew out the candles I said, "Just think Mike, in another 15 years we'll celebrate your 30th!" Michael's reply was anything but what we were expecting.

He looked up at me and our parents and very quietly replied, "I won't live to see 30. I'm already on borrowed time."

I have never forgotten those words or how I felt in that moment. Over the next five years he continued with doctors' appointments and check ups at both S. K. and L.U.H. In those five years, his health started to decline again, and it was soon discovered that another liver transplant was the answer. His body was rejecting the new one.

During this time, we didn't have faith to sustain us. We didn't know there was a GOD that could help us through this difficult journey. However, I'm thankful that we did have family who followed CHRIST and who knew how to pray for Michael, Mom, Dad and myself.

At 19 he had his second transplant and once again we were so thankful, but not quite sure who to thank or if it really mattered. Michael got better and his appointments weaned off to every six months and then finally to one a year in London.

All would be well, or so we thought. In 1988 I got engaged and plans for a spring wedding in 1989 were soon underway. It was a beautiful day in May when hubby and I said, "I do". I've always said that on that 13th day in May Stephen got the best birthday present ever. He got me!

All our families were in attendance as well as good friends. My dad wanted no one left out - 350 people were in attendance for ceremony, dinner and reception. It was like a huge family reunion on both sides.

Just four short weeks later, on June 9th at the tender age of 41, my dad passed away. We hadn't anticipated it at all. We were blindsided. As kids Michael and I would ask our dad how many Knights sat at the round table? Dad would laugh loudly and say, "Four; me, your mother,

Heather and Michael. . . Knight." Now we had lost our head Knight at the round table.

Still not having faith in GOD to help me through this stormy sea, I did what I knew best to do, put on a brave and happy face, and continue with life as though nothing was wrong. After all, I was a new bride and people lose their parents all the time. I was tough and I could handle anything.

In July hubby and I discovered that we were expecting our first baby! We were over the moon to say the least. Michael was so excited at the thought of being an uncle. Our first child, a girl, was born January 4, 1990. She missed my birthday by two hours and nineteen minutes. Baby #2, another girl, came on August 6, 1991. And finally baby #3, a boy, came January 13, 1993.

Life was busy. Life was hectic. Life was good. Life was a mess. When our son was three Stephen and I decided that I would return to work for some extra income. With only earning minimum wage and paying for day-care there really wasn't much extra income making its way into our lives.

Uncle Mike stepped up to the plate and said he would watch Little Bud as he was not in school full time yet. Our son loved his times with Uncle Mike! On one occasion I came home from work to find my son stapled to the wall by his clothing and scotch tape over his mouth! I was mortified and angry to say the least! Michael looked at me and said, "Heath, it was the only way I could keep him in one place and quiet! At least I didn't use duct tape."

We took him down off the wall, removed the tape and my son with every ounce of little boy enthusiasm said, "Mommy, Uncle Mike is the bestest taker carer of me ever!"

Every other day Uncle Mike and Lil Bud would walk into town for smokes. Uncle Mike would get Players Light and Lil Bud got Popeyes. From there they would make their way to the bench outside of the Post Office, have a smoke and watch the girls go by - Babe watchin' as it would become known as. Once again, in my life my little brother was my right arm. That was something I had told him many times in our lives, "Michael, you are my right arm!"

He would laugh and say, "I know Heath. Mom and Dad saved the best for last!" In 1999 we celebrated our son's sixth birthday with a trip to Arrowhead Park for a day of tobogganing/tubing, a pot of chilli and another one of hot chocolate. Then we went back to our house for cake and ice cream.

Uncle Mike declined to come; he wasn't feeling well. Just before Christmas (1998) Michael came down with a cold and couldn't shake it. Two months earlier Stephen took him to London for his check-up and we all thought things went well. What Michael didn't tell me, our mom or Stephen was that his body was now rejecting this liver, his organs were full of cancer from the years of the medication. Without doctors' or anyone else's knowledge Michael stopped taking all his medications and treated the pain and discomfort how he sought fit.

In the early hours of January 21, 1999, the quietness in our home was broken with the ringing of the phone. The person on the other end, a voice I did not know was frantically telling me, "He's dead. . . Mike is dead. . . You need to get here now!"

Still in somewhat of a middle-of-the-night fog, I woke up Stephen and asked him to go and check things out and he did. A couple of gut-wrenching hours later he returned and gave me the worst news ever... my baby brother, my best friend, my favorite toy, my laughing partner, my right arm, was dead!

I was devastated. I felt like my heart had been ripped out. That morning as we drove the kids to school Stephen took a different route so the kids wouldn't see all that was going on at Uncle Mike's. It would last until well into the evening.

On our way back home, I asked Stephen to go to his parents' house. I needed to be there. As we pulled into their driveway the radio started

74

playing a new hit by the band Aerosmith, "I DON'T WANT TO MISS A THING." My flood gates broke.

A few months later, I was diagnosed with a chemical imbalance that caused my ups to be way up and my lows to be extremely low, as well as depression and anxieties.

I was prescribed a strong medication and told that most likely I would be on it for the remainder of my life. If I was to go off it, I would be weened off. To just stop taking the medication could be harmful to me.

So, Heather is now a big mess! Now what do I do? I still lacked faith and I had an empty void in my heart, but I did have a praying Aunt who told me about JESUS and how HE had turned her life around and got her through some pretty dark days.

I would look at her, smile and say, "Aunty Lin I'll do the church thing when I'm old, right now while I'm young I want to have fun!" I continued to take my meds and sweep my feelings under the rug. Those that didn't fit under there I would soothe with anything that had chocolate in it. Several nights a week I went to BINGO and on weekends when the kids were at sleepovers I would drink. . . excessively!

This was the pattern for six years. During those years, in my quiet times alone, I would ask the question, "What more is there to life?" There had to be more than living a short life and then dying at the age of 29!? Remember that "borrowed time" comment Michael made on his 15th birthday? He died six months short of his 30th birthday almost to the day.

November 2004 was a time in my life that I was searching for answers to questions that I wasn't even aware I was asking. One day I bumped into Lisa, my cousin, who has always been more like a sister to me. She looked different. Her face was brighter. She had a glow about her that had never been there before. She was happier, at peace. I asked her what was going on with her. She told me that she had been going to church for the last couple of months with her mom, my Aunty Lin.

Without a moments hesitation I told her that on Sunday I wanted to go with her and check it out! That decision was amazing because that was a church, I always said I'd never step inside of. As a child there were times that I went to church with my maternal grandmother, and it was always rigid and rules oriented. That was during the 1970's. There was almost a fear of the things not understood. One of the things not understood was the Baptism of the Holy Spirit, speaking in tongues. I was told to just stay away from there.

So, I started going to church with Lisa and Aunty Lin. We went, in the evenings to Bethel Pentecostal Church in our hometown. That first night that I walked through the sanctuary doors I breathed a sigh of relief and felt like I had come home after 37 years of being away!

I had no understanding of GOD the FATHER, JESUS the SON and the HOLY SPIRIT, never mind the Baptism of the Holy Spirit! All I knew about GOD was the classic misconception that HE was this grandfather-like being who had all of these rules and if I broke even one, a lightening bolt would come down from the sky and strike me where I stood!

Religion! Who wants that? Certainly not me! But during these evening services with my "sister" and very special Aunty things started to change. I didn't know just what yet, but it was "something". On February 13, 2005, during an evening service, seated at the back of the church with Lisa and Aunty Lin, I accepted JESUS' gift of salvation and eternal life.

This was the answer to my question, "Is there more to life than living and dying!" Several months later I started going to a group called Celebrate Recovery (C.R.). It is like a 12 Step Alcoholics Anonymous. program only with C.R. When you work through a step you also work through a Beatitude. Plus, you acknowledge the "higher power" and give HIM a name, JESUS CHRIST!

It was at one of these meetings that I encountered my first, but thankfully not my last, experience where the Word of GOD actually spoke to me right there in that moment! I was reading Isaiah 41:10 and the words, "I will uphold you with my strong right arm" (paraphrased) leapt off the page and went right to my heart; my pain.

With tears streaming down my face, I turned to Lisa and said, "When Michael died, January 21, 1999, I lost my right arm, but on February 13, 2005 when I accepted CHRIST'S invitation I grew it back stronger and more victorious than before."

Today, over 17 years later, living for and with CHRIST when I think of Michael (and that's pretty much every day) I give thanks for him. I give thanks for how his passing was the pivotal moment with me answering CHRIST'S knock at the door of my heart. Until Michael's passing, I never thought about the purpose in life. When he died, I started questioning and eventually discovered JESUS is the answer.

In the first six years after Michael's death, without realizing it, I was doing a lot of soul searching. I was lost. I was missing something. I couldn't find my "north compass point". I was naive in my thinking at the time that this was just because of the loss of my little brother. It was several years later and when I had a deeper relationship with THE FATHER that I came to understand that it was actually HIM using a painful loss in my life to open my heart to Real Love, my own ROMANS 8:28 experience.

Michael may not have lived a long life, but I know I will see him again (that was another time the Word of GOD spoke to me). He will never need another transplant and he will never again have any pain or discomfort. My sorrow may have come in the night, but like it says in Psalm 30:5, my joy came in the morning. My grief found a home in the HOPE OF JESUS CHRIST AND THE STRENGTH OF HIS RIGHT ARM!

The most difficult stage of grief for me was FEELINGS OF GUILT. In the time that I was growing up it wasn't uncommon for the eldest child to be told that they were responsible for the younger one(s). That was the case in my situation. Around age eight, I was told that I was responsible for Michael. So, when he passed, I had no clue how to process that.

For the first six years after Michael died I self-medicated with alcohol and BINGO. I did my very best to put on a smile and pretend that everything was A-OKAY and I wasn't being eaten up with guilt.

I mentioned earlier, around year seven I found myself at a church group called CELEBRATE RECOVERY. Although C.R. is not a counselling ministry it did allow me to look deeper into my hurts, habits and hangups. I was able to recognize where GOD was at work in my life. By the end of the 12 steps along with the Beatitudes, with Jesus Christ in the driver's seat, I was set free from the guilt!

Another stage that I struggled with was EXPRESSING EMOTION. I simply could not put words to how or what I was feeling.

 To fight that battle I chose to talk about Michael and what I was feeling wherever and whenever despite how mixed up it might have come out. I did not apologize for it. I also applied the C.R. principles and made it thru to where the victory awaited!

If I could go back in time and talk to newly grieving Heather, I would tell her, "Do not feel guilty. You did nothing wrong; this was not your fault. There is a wonderful plan in the making, a plan that you would never believe! *Weeping may last for the night, but a shout of JOY comes in the morning."* PSALM 30:5 (NASB).

Finally, I would look straight into her eyes and with every ounce of sincerity within me I would tell her, "Heather, you will never know love and forgiveness like the love and forgiveness of Jesus Christ and you sweet girl are WORTHY of both!"

If I was to share some words with a person grieving today, I would tell them to trust in the process because you just never know what joy can come out of shear pain.

Author Bio: Heather Knight Ashby

Heather was born and raised in a small town in Muskoka. There she met and married her hubby of 34 years. She is the mom of three, two girls and one son and the proudest Nanny of the three best boys GOD ever created! Heather recently retired after 25 years from what she says was the best job ever; CROSSING GUARD. She also travels around doing Stand Up Comedy intertwined with personal testimony.

Grieving the Loss of Self

Written by Natalie Hartford

Grief is not exclusive to the death of a loved one, we can grieve the loss of self and abilities from illness.

I've always thought of myself as a strong woman. I survived an abusive childhood, the sudden death of my father at 15, and terrible teenage years followed by questionable 20's. After over 15 years of intensive therapy and a lot of work, I finally got a handle on my life. The result: my 30's were the most incredible period in my life.

Coming into my 40's with fibromyalgia would challenge everything I knew about myself.

Fibromyalgia

There is no cure. There's no known cause. It affects every person who has it differently. The National Institute of Health defines it as *"a chronic (long-lasting) disorder that causes pain and tenderness throughout the body, as well as fatigue and trouble sleeping."*

That definition, along with all the others I've come across on the web, does little to capture my experience of fibromyalgia. Every single day I'm tortured by extreme, full-body pain; chronic nausea; dizziness; blurred vision; cognitive disfunction; tinnitus; IBS; chronic, cluster migraines; insomnia; and anxiety and depression.

I've battled this condition most of my life, but in 2016 it flared up to a point where I lost everything that made me....me. I went from being a fairly active 40-year-old woman working in a career I loved, volunteering for organizations I believed in, and living my best life to an isolated, home-bound sickly woman.

In the beginning, I hung on to hope that any day, I'd find a cure and be back to my old self in no time. Little did I know, my old self was dead and gone; never to return.

Grief and illness
We often think of grief in terms of dealing with the death of a loved one. But we can grieve a divorce, miscarriage, break-up, job loss, retirement, death of a pet, or the death of a dream. Since my diagnosis of fibromyalgia, I've deeply grieved the loss of my physical, intellectual, and mental self.

Grieving the loss of my career
First was the loss of a 20+ year career in communications. In 2016, I was working for the provincial government, in a department with an agenda I was passionate about and with people I adored. I'd finally found that job everyone is looking for. The one that combined people, projects, and passion to perfection.

It was a slow death. At first, it started with two-week increments of sick leave. After four months, I had to apply for long-term disability and those notes from my doctor turned into four and six-week periods. Before I knew it, I was two years in and put on permanent disability. A year after that, I was officially terminated from my position.

My career took years of investment in education and work experience. To finally land my dream job only to have it snatched away from me by fibromyalgia has been a very painful experience.

Grieving the loss of my mind
At the same time as losing my career, I was losing my mind. It's called *fibro fog*. The term sounds so innocuous. Let me assure you, it's not. Permanently, my mind feels like I smoked three joints, drank 15 shots of tequila, took a sleeping pill, and dropped acid all at the same time.

As a writer, words, ideas, strategies, quick wit, and sharpness was my thing. My talent. My superpower. And I wore my cape with pride. I wrote thousands of words during the day at my job and thousands of words at night on my creative writing. In both my professional and creative circles, I was known for my writing prowess. I had a reputation as one of the best. It was part of me, part of my identity. Fibromyalgia and fibro fog stole that from me.

What used to take me an hour or two started to take four, six or even 12 hours until it even became impossible to pull together. Words, phrases, entire thoughts vanished in the blink of an eye, never to be found again. Story structure disappeared. Editorial ability evaporated. The ability to focus and concentrate dissolved. Every time I sat at the computer, it was a slap in the face. My disability stared back at me in the form of a blinking cursor.

I've grieved the death of the mind I once knew deeply and desperately.

Grieving the loss of friends

One of the most surprising losses has been that of many close friendships. One would assume when you get ill, your friends and family circle will support you through it. Sadly, that hasn't been the case for me and for many others I know who struggle with chronic illnesses.

Maybe people get tired of being friends with someone who chronically cancels due to illness. Maybe people get fed up with someone who doesn't *"get better."* Maybe it's hard to support someone who never improves. Maybe it's hard to know what to say or how to be a good friend in such an uncomfortable position.

I'm not entirely sure since none of them explained the eventual ghosting. All I know is my friendship circle just slowly eroded until many simply no longer existed. Grieving the loss of these friendships has been shocking and painful.

My experience with the stages of grief

Around year two, when I was in a very dark period, I realized the similarity between a lot of what I was going through and what I went through when my dad died. It dawned on me; I was grieving.

As it turned out, my experiential knowledge gave me something to lean on. I began to use what I knew about grief as a road map, to better understand how I was feeling and what to expect as I processed these losses. In fact, this became the light to my darkness. It helped me to see my illness and the losses I was facing with more compassion and patience instead of complete and utter disdain.

Putting everything I was going through in terms of grief also gave my loved ones a more tangible way to understand what I was going through along with practical things they could do to show their support.

Anger and resentment and expression of emotions

These two stages go hand-in-hand for me. The anger and resentment stage are one of the most prominent, repeating and hardest to manage stages for me. Anger feels like too tame a word to describe the emotion that takes over my body. I can feel overcome with pure, unfiltered, all-consuming rage and it can last months at a time. I want to tear my hair out, slash my body to pieces, punch, and thrash walls, demolish my kitchen table, break every dish in the house, and beat the shit out of every single person that ever sent me a "*have you tried*" message.

I haven't felt rage like this since I was a teenager and back then, I had a styrofoam wall to beat until my knuckles bled and teenage proclivities to act out my anger. I made extremely poor choices, which resulted in living with shame, guilt and self-loathing that required many years of therapy to unpack and let go of.

That's why the anger and resentment stage is the hardest for me to deal with. I have a very realistic fear that I'll revert to old coping mechanisms to deal with my anger, which could be very self-destructive. I've had to dig deep into the well to manage myself through this stage.

Years ago, kickboxing and physical pursuits were a healthy and effective outlet for my rage. However, I know my body won't be able to handle those activities now. This is where the expression of emotion stage comes into play. I find verbalizing the extent of my rage and embracing crying fits very helpful. Owning the truth of my experience instead of trying to bury it or hide it is instrumental in taming the beast.

Also, knowing this is a stage that will pass gives me patience and self-compassion. It helps keep the weight off my shoulders as I'm able to accept this is a period I'm going though and although it feels like it'll last forever, it won't.

Depression and loneliness

The other stage that plays on repeat for me is depression and loneliness. Understandably, in the beginning, I went through a period of deep depression. I practically lived in a zero-gravity chair for months on end, nearly comatose.

Living with a chronic illness feels very isolated and lonely. No one else can truly know or understand what I'm feeling, even others with fibro. During times of intense loneliness, I must fight the urge to turn even further inward. To detach, disconnect and insulate my internal bubble where it feels weirdly safe. But I've learned this only compounds and heightens depression and loneliness.

During these periods, I try to talk to my doctor more openly about my mental state, consider medication changes when appropriate, and seek therapy. I up my self-care game with reading, meditation, restorative yoga, and Reiki treatments. Also, reminding myself *"this is a stage"* can give me the courage and strength to hang on, sometimes by my fingernails, as I come through the other side.

Also, in the last few years, I've started investing in deepening my connection with a very small inner circle of friends, some of whom also suffer with a chronic illness, to create a support group of sorts. Along with their being a text or phone call away, we schedule two or three weekend trips to cottages each year where we actively support one other.

While part of those weekends is for laughs and scrabble, we also make an active and purposeful effort to have raw and honest confessional type talks so we can offer each other non-judgmental support. Surrounding myself with a small group of people I trust, who are compassionate and who truly understand, helps me process loneliness in a healthy environment.

Panic and overwhelm

As I was working through accepting my diagnosis, I asked my doctor how I'm supposed to live the next 40+ years like this. How am I supposed to get up and walk through life, find happiness, and live fully knowing this is my past, present and future? There's no cure, no magic pill, and no relief around the corner.

I have to fight every day not to let that knowledge lead me down a rabbit hole of panic and overwhelm. And in the beginning, it often did. If I think about it too much or live in *"worst case scenario land"* for too long, I can lose myself in heart palpitations and paralyzing anxiety.

For me, acceptance has been the balm to panic and overwhelm. It's about learning to be ok with not being ok. Every. Single. Day. It's about not resisting. It's about leaning IN. And in leaning in, I find space to acknowledge my new truth and reality and turn my focus to redefining myself, my dreams, my expectations, and my goals.

Feelings of guilt

For me, I deal with an incredible amount of guilt around letting people down. For example, in 2019 I missed all my husband's birthday celebrations; the family dinner and an awards banquet where he was being honoured. I was devastated to miss out and felt incredible guilt that I let him down. That I disappointed him.

Those types of situations present themselves in some shape or form every single day. I constantly need to change or adjust plans and therefore some loved one is always getting told, *"No, I can't. I'm sorry."* But guilt is a poison and it'll crush me where I stand with its negativity if I let it.

I'm learning to let go of it by focusing on the joy I receive watching the people I love do fun things and have grand experiences, even if it's without me. I also work persistently at monitoring my self-talk. I can fall into a pit of self-loathing pretty quickly when I feel like I'm letting my loved ones down. I fight against this by practicing active self-compassion through self-acceptance, self-awareness, mindfulness, and gratitude.

Does it still suck? Yes. Are my friends and family sometimes sad or disappointed when I can't take part? Absolutely. But we've all had to work hard at accepting my limitations and celebrating the wins when we get them. And I'm realizing how important it is to be honest with the people who love me about what I am or am not able to do at any particular time. It is getting easier with time and practice.

Hope comes through and we find a new reality

For me, these two stages go together. This is where I've found myself for the last year. I'm in a place where I'm at peace with what is. My anger is quiet. My depression is manageable. Shock, denial, and guilt seem muted. I've made friends with my new reality. Acceptance has been key in getting me here.

When I first started on this journey, my pain shrink told me acceptance was integral to getting to the best place I could be. I was instantly frustrated and pissed! How do I accept my new reality? Isn't acceptance sort of like giving up? How do I accept being a shadow of who I was after I worked so hard to get there?

If I accept what is, right here, right now what does that mean for my life? What does it mean for my marriage and the lifestyle we worked so hard to enjoy? What does it mean for my work, my career, my independence?

That's when I realized acceptance wasn't the enemy. Acceptance is about finding a way to live with adversity, to sit with struggle and find a way to live your best life regardless. Acceptance is acknowledging your truth, honouring your pain and struggle, understanding your limitations, and then redefining yourself, your dreams, your expectations, and your goals. It's about not resisting. It's about leaning IN.

Through acceptance I've been able to achieve a better balance of doing things that are important to me and that I love while also ensuring time to rest, listening to my body, and taking care of myself. There is room for improvement, and I know it'll go up and down, but now that I know acceptance isn't the enemy and doesn't mean giving up, I just keep trying.

Again, knowing this is a stage and understanding that I can whip in and out of stages like Cybil, I know it is important to maximize this peaceful time; to make the most of it. It may last a long time. It may not.

If you are grieving, here's what I'd like you to know
Just when I think I'm coming out the other side of grief, I can find myself going through one, two or all the stages of grief again at different phases of my life. But it gets easier and more manageable as my experience with it grows. That said, there are things I've found that help mitigate and soften the sharp edges of grief.

Learning to say no
Like many people, I struggle with saying no. I'm a people pleaser. I want everyone to be happy. I hate to disappoint. Saying no has also received the most push back. Likely because people aren't used to me saying "no," cancelling plans or being unavailable for long stretches of time.

The truth of the matter is some people don't get it. And they never will. No matter what I say or how I explain it, they'll never fully appreciate or understand what I'm living with. Part of acceptance is realizing that's okay. I don't need them to.

I've learned the most important thing I can do is honour myself and my needs and let others deal with their own feelings however they choose to. It's not my job to make them feel better. It's not my job to console them or help them understand. It's my job to take care of myself!

Gratitude

I've learned when facing life's biggest challenges like grief and chronic illness, then more than ever, I need to remind myself of the good, daily. When so much has been taken away or lost, taking time to appreciate what I have can feel like the hardest thing to do. That's how I know it's incredibly vital to my mental health.

It takes active effort to turn off the negative thinking so I can see the wins. So, I started with super small wins. Getting out of bed, win. Taking a bath, win. Walking the dogs, big win. Washing my hair, win. Smiling, win. Putting on pants with a button and zipper, win.

I started by writing every win down in a journal to ingrain my new focus and way of thinking into my psyche. Slowly but surely, the good grew and became more central to my focus. Whenever I re-enter a stage of grief, I pull this coping mechanism out of my bag of tricks, and it always helps lessen the intensity.

Authenticity and honesty

For the first few years, I hid how I was doing from everyone. When asked how my health was, I'd answer with some version of *"fine"*. Part of me didn't believe they really wanted the truth. I figured they were asking to be polite. And we all know no one likes a complainer and that's what it felt like when I was honest. Also, part of me didn't really know how to verbalize the true extent of what I was going through. And it was exhausting to try. Often *"fine"* was just easier.

But denying my truth made me feel like a liar and pretender. Not to mention, I realized a critical component to accepting my new reality was no longer downplaying how I was doing.

So, I took the time to learn a new language around my illness, losses, and grief so I could appropriately share my experience with others. I spent some of my darkest days doing body scans and journaling about every sensation I was feeling. Trying out different verbs, adjectives, and expressions to find things that felt accurate.

Then when asked how I was, I had a vocabulary to draw from enabling me to be honest and authentic about my reality.

- *"I've been struggling with a pain flare for the last few weeks that makes my blood feel like liquid nitrogen pumping through my veins. It sucks, but I'm hoping it passes soon. Thanks for caring enough to ask."*
- *"Today my pain is humming so intensely it feels like an electrical current. It's so strong, I feel like I might levitate. No, there's nothing you can do, but I really appreciate you listening."*
- *"While I know I look ok, I've been in a chronic nausea flare for months that has me dry heaving all day. Ugh. Nothing worse, but I'm finding new protein smoothies to be a lifesaver. It means a lot that you asked."*

My experience has been by accepting my truth and expressing it authentically, it's created the opportunity for more meaningful conversations that have deepened some of my relationships and allowed me to truly educate people about fibromyalgia. It's also given people who care about me the chance to truly support me because they're now in the truthful know.

For those who it might make uncomfortable, they can stop asking.

Setting boundaries

Setting personal boundaries is hard for me, much like saying no. As part of accepting my current reality, I let go of toxic relationships. First, I regularly filter my social networks blocking anyone who perpetuates negativity. Second, I limit my time on social networks, especially when I'm in a dark place. And finally, I don't make time for those who aren't healthy for me.

The result is my chosen social circle is a lot smaller. But now the energy I do have for activities is invested in those who matter most; those who love me unconditionally and are ok if they don't see me for weeks or even months or if I cancel and reschedule plans a hundred times. The experience has been quite liberating. I highly recommend it.

Maintaining hobbies and interests

For me, this has meant looking at activities that I can keep doing with alterations and investigating and trying out new interests. Writing this article, for example, has been incredibly difficult and time-consuming. I've had to pace myself, work in many starts and stops, and just accept that if I'd like to write, I need to do it differently. And while the changes aren't easy, the result is something that's brought me immense satisfaction and pride in doing. So, it's worth it.

While doing agility with my dogs brought me incredibly joy, I had to give it up because it required a lot of running and physical coordination. Instead, I started doing scent training with them. It's significantly less taxing on my body but brings me the same level of joy from working and training with them.

Keeping invested in activities that bring me joy is hard to maintain through stages like depression and anger or if I'm in a fibro flare, so I give myself permission to take breaks when needed and come back to things when I'm in a better head space. Knowing it doesn't ever have to be all or nothing is key.

In conclusion

In the end, grief is something all of us will face in our lifetime. Knowing how to recognize it in yourself and others will ensure you have the know-how to support yourself and loved ones in the healthiest and best ways you can.

Author Bio: Natalie Hartford

Born in Scarborough, Ontario, Natalie has lived in New Brunswick since she was six months old. First in Moncton, then the Miramichi, finally settling in Fredericton in 1993. She graduated with a Bachelor of Applied Arts in Journalism from St. Thomas University and attained a Diploma in Print Journalism from the New Brunswick Community College, graduating with highest academic standings.

After completing her education, she proceeded to spend close to 20 years working as a Communications Specialist for a variety of not-for-profits along with several federal and provincial government departments. She also put her writing and marketing talents to work volunteering for many Fredericton organizations such as MADD Canada (Fredericton chapter), Meals on Wheels Fredericton, March the Trail of Dimes and Family Enrichment and Counselling.

In her spare time, she enjoys creative writing of all sorts, reading, restorative yoga and anything outdoors.

In 2016, she was forced into medical retirement when her fibromyalgia become unmanageable. Since then, she's been working hard to adjust to a new, quieter lifestyle with her husband and two precocious Nova Scotia Duck Tolling Retrievers.

Grieving is a Process

Written by May Atkinson

Grieving is a process. It has no time limit or schedule. It can start before we physically lose someone or after they've died.

Whether we lose someone who has been struggling with health issues, or it happens unexpectedly; it still hurts either way.

What we have known for years, and maybe took for granted is now gone.

Faith is how I deal with it. We are all passing through this world to our next.

My grief started when both my dad and my mom died within five months apart. It was February 2006, already a busy time for our family as my daughter was a contestant in the Miss Woodstock pageant. Mom was admitted into the ICU on life support. While we were concerned about losing her; our dad passed away very unexpectedly.

Even though they had been separated for over 20 years, they still had a bond. They were friends. So, we were concerned about telling Mom that Dad had passed. It turned out that Mom had a dream, and she knew. She "had a feeling", she told us, that dad would not be here when the time came for her to be discharged from the hospital. She knew he was gone before we told her.

Strength, I believe, comes from faith, family, and friends.

We feel we got a second chance with Mom. God gave us a gift of another five months with her. Mom was our rock not only when we were going through things with Dad's death, but every step of the way.

We moved to New Brunswick from Connecticut in 1971. We left what we knew. Disagreements with my spouse always resulted in a call to my mom. Then, when she passed, I was with her the night before. In the morning my brother walked by, and gently kissed her forehead. Shortly after she said "It's time to go..." But oh, how I wanted to grasp those last few moments. I held off as long as I dared before calling the ambulance to go to the hospital. She knew, I knew...she would not be coming home again.

I believe that people die at a certain time, for a reason. Sometimes we blame ourselves. "I should have ..." OR "I shouldn't have..." Once we realize there was nothing we could have done, we can get through that stage of grief.

I believe God gives us each a teacup saucer. Through life we add to it, and it becomes a bread plate. Then we add more, and our life becomes a dinner plate. In 2006, I had a full platter with sideboards!! I was not sure how I would make it through, but over time and trust in God, my platter slowly went back to being the dinner plate and then a bread plate.

We can handle everything that comes our way with faith and trust in God. At times we don't see how we can handle things. But remember they happen for a reason. Our job is not to know why, but to trust...It does get better and lighter.

Even with faith we need to allow ourselves to grieve. There is no time limit. Allow yourself to cry, and I mean cry!! From deep inside, where it hurts the most.

Allow yourself time to reminisce on what was.
Anger – Yes –Anger is also a part of grieving. Allow yourself to feel this too. Give yourself space; what we knew has changed and in a way we now have too.

In less than three years, I lost my father, who I adored, my mother, who was my best friend, my mother-in-law who accepted me with open arms into her family for over 25 years, and a grandmother (who fought death). Three years ago we said goodbye to my father-in-law, whom thought of me as his own daughter. And less than six months ago, Phyllis, who thought of me as her "chosen" daughter. Each of these individuals played a different role in my life, but similar, each loved and believed in me.

Death, if we allow it, can be beautiful. I know that does not sound right but think about it. The person is entering eternity...forever!! "Till we meet again."

With each passing it does not become easier, I have learned to accept that life changes and this is part of it.

Phyllis and I talked a lot. I told her about when mom passed, how she said goodbye to each of her children, and I believe she also chose the day.

With Phyllis we shared many conversations about life, children, traveling, faith, family, and the importance of each. I took away so much each time. She taught me to always try your best and accept life as it is. Spend quality time with your significant other, even if it's a cup of coffee or time at an old camp. She asked me many times why she was still here, I reassured her that God was not done yet, with her journey here, and there was still work to be done.

The day of her passing... I knew.... She knew... We didn't say it, but we knew. We shared tears, hugs, and peace. The day was so serene. Quiet. When she asked me to call "her boys", I did not hesitate. I knew what she wanted...to say goodbye.

When they came with their wives she was in her happy place. She spoke with each of them, it was very important they each knew how much she loved them. And she did her best with what she knew to be their mom.

After they all left…I sat beside her, she was unresponsive by this time. But I know she could hear, I told her the day was perfect, the boys got along just like she wanted. We all enjoyed supper together. "And most of all you got to tell each one of them that you loved them".

I told her it was now her time, and it was okay to go. I told her that all is well and will be well. It wasn't 10 minutes until she took her final breath…she was finally free from the pain she had; she could breathe again. She was with Clair, her husband, whom I know she missed dearly through our conversations.

I feel people need to know they are loved. They have done their best and have kept their faith and so much more awaits.

I told this to my brothers-in-law when their mom was passing. Each spoke quietly with her letting her know she was much loved and very much appreciated. She too went peacefully.

"I have fought the good fight. I have finished the race; I have kept the faith" 2 Timothy 4:7 (NIV).

We too need to know that we have done our best. There is no blame. We cannot go back and change what we did or didn't do. We take what we know and move forward.

So, when Phyllis passed; again, I lost my best friend, confidant and "my other mom" She was my "chosen mom". She had told my mom that she adopted me as her "chosen daughter" years ago.

I gave thanks for her and knew she was where she belonged.

I hold onto the verse *"Be still and know that I am God"* Psalm 46:10 (NIV). It speaks so loudly if we listen.

The lyrics in the Patti Loveless song, "How Can I Help You Say Goodbye" says a lot. We played this at our mom's funeral.

Author Bio: May Atkinson

May was born in Hartford, Connecticut and moved to New Brunswick in 1971. Raised on the family's potato farm along with her four siblings in Jackson Falls, NB. She learned the importance of family, the simple things in life, and love for the outdoors.

She now lives in Richmond Corner, NB with her husband Ernest for over 35 years. Mother of two, a daughter and son and Grammy of four.

She has spent many years volunteering within her community organizing events at the Richmond Corner Recreation Center where many memories and friendships have been built.

As busy as she can be, she always finds time for what's most important to her; family and friends. Down time you will find her in the kitchen baking cookies with her grandchildren, four-wheeling, and spending time at the family camp on First Eel River Lake.

May currently works in Houlton, Maine.

Don't Fight the Curve

Written as told by Michelle Maguire

To say that life can throw you a few curve balls is an understatement. It's all how you take the pitch that determines how you will score.

When I look at my life and the different traumas I have gone through, I had no choice other than to learn how to accept and navigate through them. Never did I realize that each of these navigations were part of grief. The grieving process comes in all different ways and can sometimes be short and other times take a long time to get through it. Processing grief is not easy, and it is something that we can and will encounter at all stages of our lives. I hope that by sharing my story, I will help others know that what they are feeling is normal and that they are not alone.

It started when I decided to leave my marriage six years ago. This was one of the hardest decisions that I had to make in my life because my decision was not only going to affect me, but it was also going to affect my children. It was also not what I envisioned for our lives, but the alternative of staying was not healthy for any of us.

A little over a year-and-a-half into my marriage my first son was born, and life was good. We were happy and navigating our lives as a newly married couple and as new parents. We faced ups and downs like any new couple did until my son turned 15 months old, and this is where things began to change.

Both my ex-husband and I were diagnosed with cancer, within a month of each other. Not at all what we expected and so many emotions and fears that raged through us. How were we going to get through this? Were we going to be here for our son? This wasn't supposed to happen. The next year was hell. It was hard trying to raise a 15-month-old baby, treatment, working full-time and trying to cope with this double whammy. It put some stress on our marriage.

My ex-husband was withdrawn and quiet. He didn't want to talk about what we were going through, whereas being a Mom I just had to keep going because we had a child, and someone needed to make sure he was nurtured.

God and faith really helped me during this difficult time. I did question a lot. I turned away from the church for a little while because I was very angry with God. I kept asking, "Why is my life like this? Did I do something wrong? Life was not supposed to be this way."

I can remember being told during that year that we might not be able to have any more children. Then, on Christmas morning that following year, we found out I was pregnant with my second son. He was truly a miracle. Life started to get better again for a little while until my husband started having some issues with depression. He became reclused. He pulled away from the kids and me and that was the beginning of the end. Trouble at work changed him to different shifts which took him away from us more. We began to struggle financially and there were days I didn't know what I was going to come home to. I can remember multiple times trying to reach him and no answer. I no longer knew the man that I had fallen in love with. Trying to navigate a failing marriage while raising two children was very challenging and I was afraid to leave because I didn't know if I could do this on my own and that's not what my life was supposed to be like.

I didn't want to be a stereotype. I didn't want my children to be looked at differently because they had divorced parents. After a few years of living in this toxic environment, family and friends became our support system and gave me the courage that I needed to leave. I can remember a good friend looking after the boys, making them feel special and was a positive role model for them. He showed us the happiness that we were missing in our lives and provided me with the encouragement that I needed to do what was best for the boys and me. As he was helping me, I had no idea that he was going through struggles of his own and 10 months later, he took his own life.

Talk about shock and an area of unfamiliar territory. Dealing with the grief of divorce, raising children alone and now a close friend taking his own life, it was a lot to take in. I was faced with so many stages of grief all at once. There was so much going on, including helping my children grieve and navigate all these curve balls. At that time my focus was on everyone else, but me.

I thank God every day for my parents and their support. My dad stepped into roles that he shouldn't have but he did, and he was the male role model for my boys. He went to every game and school event and did everything he could to keep the boys on the straight and narrow since they didn't have their father in their lives. Things were good and then here comes the next curve ball, my dad was diagnosed with terminal cancer in June of 2019. I found myself navigating my dad's treatments, my mom and my sons dealing with the diagnosis, and the uncertainties while trying to stay positive. It was not easy!

In 2020, during Covid, my dad passed away and our world crumbled. At that point I had to take a step back and try to focus. I remember sitting in a room and once again straying from my faith because I was angry, looking up to ask God, "What is happening? Why is this all happening to me? It is not fair. Haven't we been through enough?"

It wasn't until I lost my dad, I took the time to grieve. We were hit with one thing after the next and I had to keep going for my family. I was in shock and emotional and I was short-fused more than I should have been. It was a lot!

I kept myself very involved in things because I wanted to stay busy, so people didn't know what I was going through. While going through all of this I was the PTA President, I was the Room Mom, I was the Team Mom, and I coached my kids' sports. I did everything I could to paint a perfect picture. That was my mask, so I didn't have to acknowledge what I was going through and feel the pain of what was needed to be felt. I was in denial, and I was stuck here for a while.

I felt panicked and overwhelmed so many times and asked myself 100 times over, "Where do I go from here? How am I raising two young men with no male figure in their lives? How am I helping my mom get through this? How am I going to get through this?" My main thing was that I didn't want my boys to think life has to suck all the time. We can go through bad things, and we can find a way to get through it.

For a good portion of the time, I felt guilt. I felt like I was a failure. I had failed in my marriage. I had failed my boys and I was stuck here for a long time.

Looking back and at the big picture, I realize now it wasn't my fault. You can't fix someone who doesn't want to help himself. I wanted a better life for my boys and myself and we deserved it.

In January 2021, I started working with a Life Coach. That's when I started to break down and deal with the feelings of guilt, and anger. I am still angry with my ex-husband because we have these two wonderful boys, and he doesn't have anything to do with them. They literally saved me from spiralling down into a dark space. They've taught me and encouraged me. They keep pushing me to do more.

In March 2021, I realized mentally I was getting into a good place so then I needed to do something for my physical self. I had been very good at being empathetic to everybody else, so now it was time to have empathy for myself and forgive myself.

I have lost 65 pounds and still going. I have started coaching others in two different areas. Those that are overweight and looking for a physical solution and those have gone through divorce and trauma. I want to give back because the feelings of being stuck, alone and that I had no one to turn to and feelings of being judged because you're not "okay," are things that I don't want other people to feel.

My kids are my driving force. They tell me I'm not failing and that I have provided them with everything that I could. I have filled roles of mom and dad and have led them to be strong and secure. I have provided them with a quality education via catholic and private school and I have not allowed them to become victims of the system because their dad choses to ignore his obligations. I am living proof that you can survive, and you can navigate loss, grief and recreate your identity. I know that I am not alone, and I want others to realize they are not alone.

Grief sucks but if I didn't go through what I've went through, I wouldn't be where I'm at in my life right now. When we grieve, people look at us and think we're strong, but internally we have things we're dealing with. It is scary, but it's all part of the process and unfortunately, we will go through it many times throughout our lives. It's how we deal with it.

Now, I'm preparing to head into another stage of life this fall, where my oldest son is going to college. I'm going to miss him, and I know another stage of grief is going to start all over again. This is a different type of grief where I'm happy for him but scared. The positive is that I know I have the experience and knowledge to section things off and process it differently.

I've learned that I must trust myself because things can get out of control. I also have faith, and whatever that looks like for you will help a lot. Don't ever give up -your story is filled with many chapters and your chapter can change at any moment.

A few takeaways... Don't ever be afraid to tell your story because you don't know how your story will help someone else. There are many people out there who need to hear your story and be careful not to lose yourself in the process.

When you go through these different challenges a lot of times, we tend to put ourselves to the back burner because, that's the way "it is supposed to be." It is important to have someone who can hold an open space for you and listen to you. I didn't think I needed "therapy" per se but I needed someone to listen and give me a different perspective. Support from your community is so important.

If I were able to go back and talk to myself when I was first grieving, I would say, "Take a breath, don't be afraid and know that things will be okay. You will not be in this season forever." At the time it doesn't feel like things are going to be okay, but they will. You may feel like you're never going to get through the grief, but you will, and you will grow from it. "Allow yourself to process your grief and don't feel guilty or that you have failed... you haven't. Failure is your way to finding success."

What I'd like to leave with you is, embrace the challenges, feel the pain, don't be afraid to fail and know you're not alone. Life is going to throw you curve balls, it's how you hit the pitch that will get you to home plate.

Author Bio: Michelle Maguire

Michelle Maguire holds a true passion for helping others transform and meet their goals in all facets of their lives. She has experienced multiple life-changing events which have led to self-discovery and a beautiful life changing transformation that encourages others that anything is possible.

Michelle is a single mother of two teenage sons, Michael, and Matthew, who she cherishes and has devoted her life to providing them love and opportunities to make them successful, while managing a full-time leadership career in the healthcare industry for over 20 years.

Most recently, Michelle has fulfilled her passion in writing and helping others. In 2022, Michelle became a #1 International Best-Selling Author for her very first multi author book and has hit multiple Best-Selling Lists for her second. She also became an independent life and health coach who continues to inspire and help others achieve their goals and dreams.

Michelle is excited to pay it forward and is thankful for the life lessons she has learned throughout her journey. She believes that her transformation would not have been possible without those lessons. It is her hope that by sharing her story and experiences you will know that you are not alone, and that with the right mindset and inspiration, life changing transformations are possible. She looks forward to working with you to help you reach your goals.

Facebook Group: fb.me/*michellemaguirecoaching*
Instagram: www.instagram.com/*michellemaguirecoaching*
Instagram handle is @michellemaguirecoaching

Don't Give Up

Written by Simon MacInnis

My first experience with grief was when I found out my mom was diagnosed with cancer in 1982. She died in May 1983.

I felt blindsided by Mom's death. One morning Dad told us he had to take Mom to the hospital, and she would be there a few days. A couple days later a friend and I went to the hospital after school to see her. The nurse checked on her and came and told us that she was sleeping so we couldn't go in.

Many years later I found out that Dad had left instructions with the staff that my brother and I were not allowed in to see her because she was hooked up to life support and other wires. He didn't want us to be traumatized nor did he want our last memory of Mom to be like that.

I remember being at the funeral home when the visitation of my mom was about to end. I was kneeling on the prayer bench in front of Mom's casket. I was crying. My uncle came and put his arm around me. He said, "Everything is going to be okay." That uncle has been a great support to me.

That was a really tough year for me. I was 10 and my brother was 9. I got the German Measles twice that year, so I missed a lot of school due to health reasons. Then, add on top of that my mom passed away.

Not only did I lose my mom that year, but I lost a lot of my friends because the school held me back a year. All my friends went on to a different school, being in Intermediate. I was left in the same school with my younger friends. I was really upset with the school system for doing that to me. Even though I went to the same school as my friends the next year I didn't really catch up to my friends until we went to high school.

I began to battle depression. It is an ongoing part of my life. I essentially have a gap, where I grew up without my mom. Initially, when Mom passed away, I had a really hard time. I had been raised to go to church but after Mom died, I rebelled against God and the church. I went off the rails.

There were several times when Dad got home from work at the end of the day, and I wasn't home. A neighbor who was a police officer gave me a ride home —not because I was in trouble or broke the law, but because he saw me hanging out on the street and offered me a ride home.

Living in a small community provided me with a great support system. After a while, my friends started coming around and saying, "This isn't the Simon we grew up with. We know you're going through a hard time, and we want to be here to support you."

There was no grief counselling. We just had to pick up the pieces and go on with our lives. Looking back, I realize I watched Dad become the strong person that he always was. For about two years it was just the three of us, my dad, my brother, and I. Dad had to raise two boys on his own and he still had his full-time job. He was still involved in the community and with students. We saw that he cared so much that it trickled over to us.

Looking back, I wonder if I have difficulty today because I wasn't given grief counselling when Mom died; I wasn't given the time to process things and grieve well.

When I was in seventh grade, I started putting pieces together and I started going back to my Christian upbringing.

At school we sang Oh Canada and said the Lord's Prayer. During the prayer I would lay my head on my desk. One day my seventh-grade teacher asked me to stay late after school and he would give me a ride home. I thought I was in trouble.

He said, "I really feel like you're missing something in your life."

I replied to him, "No kidding! You think I'm missing something? I'm missing my mom!"

He said he understood I was missing my mom, but he said he felt I was missing something else. He invited me to come to the Inter Varsity Christian Fellowship. He said I could come, and I didn't have to say anything. I could sit in the back, and I didn't even have to introduce myself.

So, I started going to that group and that is when I started to connect the dots and go back to my Christian upbringing. I think I didn't really process my grief. I understood Mom was gone and I just had to get on with my life as if it was normal.

At the end of 7th grade my dad married Janet, who has become my second Mom ever since then. She was the mother figure in my life as I went into adolescence.

For a while I didn't see her as my mom, but she said, "I never want to replace your mom. I just want to be here for your family." Now, I see her as my mom.

When I went to junior high, in 8th grade Janet officially adopted my brother and I. It was really just paperwork of something that had already been in place for a while.

I feel like I will always have a gap for the time that I didn't really grieve my mom's death. However, having Jesus Christ as my center really helped me through this difficult time. My support system of friends really helped as well.

The next experience of grief for me was seeing my dad's health decline and then his eventual passing. His health started to decline about 2002. It was hard to see Dad give up his driver's license and watch his independence wither away.

Watching the journey he had with Multiple Sclerosis, I watched him go from walking with a cane, to a walker, then to a wheelchair and finally he was bedridden.

When 2017 came I made multiple flights from my home in Newfoundland to see my dad in New Brunswick. Many times, I would be on my way home and I'd get a call that Dad wasn't going to make it, so I needed to turn around and go back to Dad.

One time I had just landed in Halifax, and I got a call from the hospital that his time had come. So, I was in Halifax, and I literally went up the arrival stairs, and into the bathroom to change into a fresh set of clothes. Then I turned around and went to departures to fly back to New Brunswick.

When I made the last trip in 2018, I think I knew I might not get another trip back before Dad died. I made peace with God before Dad died.

It was hard for me when he actually did die, because he died during Covid, on May 25th, 2020. Three days prior to Dad's death the Atlantic Bubble closed. That meant that if I flew to New Brunswick, I would have to quarantine for 14 days when I arrived and I would have to quarantine for another 14 days when I arrived home.

Essentially, it would be a month of isolation from my family. That wasn't feasible so I wasn't able to go to my dad's funeral. I didn't have the closure of the visitation, funeral, and graveside services. I helped with arrangements by inviting people to the visitation and the graveside services and contacting my dad's two sisters to write the obituary. I did what I could from Newfoundland.

It was difficult not having the closure of those services. During the summer of 2022 I was able to visit Dad's grave. I believe that is when I finally started to get closure.

Going forward I know someday my mom, Janet will die, so I will essentially lose 3 parents. My father-in-law's health is not well, so I know I will have grief when he passes.

I have also been through a recent grief. Through massive amounts of prayer, Bible reading, counselling, and learning to be present I have been able to rectify the situation.

Looking back, I realize the three stages of grief that were most difficult for me were the State of Shock, Expressing Emotion and Depression & Loneliness. I thought it was so unfair that my mother died at such a young age. Then I realized that there have been so many breakthroughs in medicine that her death contributed to perhaps helping some future generation. Had they known more about cancer back then she may still be alive today.

I experienced panic and overwhelm on the first day after each of my parents passed. I was a bit angry that I wasn't able to go to my dad's funeral, but I wasn't angry about his death.

I did have anger and resentment about my mom's passing.

Christ is my hope and my center and that's what kept me going. I had to find a new reality without my parents. I still have my mom, -Janet- who I continue to check in on.

If I were to travel back in time to my former self I would tell him, "It's going to be okay. There's going to be dark times and happy times. You're going to struggle, but you're going to get through it."

To people who are grieving today I would encourage you by saying "Don't give up. Don't give in to the struggle. There's going to be good days and there's going to be bad days. Remember that nothing that you do, other than moving forward, is going to change the fact that you're dealing with this grief, whether it's a divorce, death of a pet, or death of a loved one."

Author Bio: Simon MacInnis

Simon hails originally from Calgary, Alberta, but grew up in the Maritimes (Woodstock, NB and Moncton, NB).

He now lives in Conception Bay South, Newfoundland, with his wife Donna (Tilley) and their three daughters: Emilee aged 7, Eve aged 5, and Ella aged 3. They also have two dogs: a Chihuahua named Allie and a Mastador (Lab mix) named Nova.

Simon is a veteran of the Canadian Armed Forces and has also worked in the field of Occupational Health and Safety for 15 years. He is a graduate of Kingswood University, where he obtained his Bachelor of Arts/Religion with a major in Youth Ministry.

Simon is the host of a podcast called "The Journey of Faith" https://www.facebook.com/faithjourneypodcast.

Broken But Still Standing
Written by Pam Drost

Suicide -it is a word that brings chills to my body because I lost my son Jason to it in August 2020. He was 49 years old. Jason had two sons.

Jason was a hard-working man who provided for his wife and two boys. He could fix anything that was broken -except for himself. He had two failed marriages.

Both wives were unfaithful to him, but he carried on. He supported his boys and taught them about hard work and how to make a good life for themselves. All he ever wanted out of life was to have a life partner who loved him as much as he loved them. But it wasn't meant to be.

Then Covid hit and he got laid off from his job as a licenced red seal plumber. He also experienced another broken relationship.

He was a talented, self-taught guitar player. When he and his last girlfriend broke up he had no where to go, so we let him stay at our cottage, at Davidson Lake. It was there that he took his life.

One Thursday we visited him at the cottage. He didn't think he was very good at singing, but he enjoyed playing the guitar. That Thursday he played his guitar. He and I had some great conversations.

The next week one of his sons called him and didn't get an answer. He later texted him and didn't get a reply. After awhile he contacted his brother and asked him, "Have you heard from Dad this week?"

When he replied that he'd reached out but hadn't received any replies the boys decided to go to the cabin to check on him. Unfortunately, they found he'd taken his life.

It has been the hardest thing my husband and I have had to go through. I'll never forget that night when his oldest son, Auston, called and said his dad was gone.

Suicide leaves the loved ones with a lot of questions. Why did Jason commit suicide at our cottage where we had so many good memories? Did he reach out to God before he died? What happened to his soul? Is it lost forever? Why didn't he reach out for help to us or to a mental health counselor? Did he have a physical ailment we didn't know about?

I know it's a sin to take your life and I worry that his soul may be lost. Some people in our church family say he may have asked God for forgiveness before he died. I pray that is so.

Without God in our lives, I don't know how we would have made it through. God is the answer to many who are struggling if they would only open their hearts to him. Thank God we did.

Psalm 139:10 (KJV) *"Even there shall thy hand lead me, and thy right hand shall hold me."*

God is holding us now and forever.

Author Bio: Pam Drost

Pam lives in Southampton, New Brunswick with her husband. They have lived there almost 45 years. They have been married for 54 years. They had four boys and now three.

Pam has worked at a variety of jobs over the years. Site interpreter at Kings Landing for seven years, supplied at all three Nackawic schools as a janitor, supply teacher and teacher's aide. Pam also worked at a special care home near Fredericton. She also kept books for their trucking company until she retired.

Pam enjoys reading, doing puzzles, gardening, and spending time at our cottage at Davidson Lake. She also enjoys quilting with the Comfort Quilters at the Nackawic Wesleyan Church. They donate their quilts to people who have cancer and other serious illnesses.

Heaven Is Real

By Diana [Aitken] Manuel

I believe each of us deals with grief differently and there is no right or wrong way. Looking back, I can see that my grief, or the bulk of it was dealt with in the months leading up to my husband's death.

Here is my story...

At 43 years old I found myself a widow and alone. My husband died at the age of 44, our daughter was married and our son in university.

Approximately two years previous it all started with a mole on his back that was melanoma. Being the 90's, we didn't have a computer or Google, so we just knew they had got it all during surgery and he didn't need any treatment.

Just over a year later it reared its ugly head again. This time it was as a visible lump the size of an orange in his left armpit. Again, surgery got it all. Our shock was when the oncologist told us there would be no treatment as it could have already spread and could lay dormant for up to 10 years.

We were told we had a choice —we could worry daily about it coming back, or we could enjoy every day to the fullest. We chose to enjoy every day! Six months later, a lump appeared on the left side of his neck. We were shocked to find out it was sitting on his carotid artery, and no one would attempt surgery.

This, I believe, is when I began to grieve. My husband lost his quality of life and retreated within himself only to say, "I have lived a good life. I know where I'm going. I just wish I didn't have to die to get there."

During this time, I found great comfort in Psalm 91. I read it often out loud, making it personal by inserting my name in each verse.

Together, we planned his Celebration of Life. He chose his pallbearers, his Disney character tie (to make people smile), and the song, "When I Get to Heaven", which his chosen soloist sang for him before he passed. He also requested that the message of salvation be given and that John 3:16 KJV (For God so loved the world, that he gave his only begotten Son, that whosoever believeth in him should not perish, but have everlasting life,) be on his tombstone. I believe doing these things together helped me grieve.

In the scriptures it says, "You do not receive because you do not ask," so I made a request of my husband before he died. "If it is possible," I said, "and if heaven is a real place, would you please ask God to send an eagle to our deck. That will let me know you arrived safely." After I asked my husband that, I told my daughter and my pastor what I had asked.

Then early one morning my husband and I were talking about the day. Just as I went to leave the room, I heard a slight sound. I turned around and he was gone. Talking one moment and gone the next! The tumor had finally cut off his carotid artery. As I went to him, I had the most unbelievable experience as I felt his spirit leave his body and linger in the room. He was watching me! It was totally amazing! It brought me great comfort during that difficult time.

Within a week of his passing my daughter was sitting at the kitchen table by the patio doors. Our pastor and his wife were also there. Suddenly my daughter shouted "Mom!"

I ran to her and looked out the patio door. There was a bald-headed eagle, about eight feet off the deck floor. With its wingspan between the house and the deck railing, it flew the 30-foot length of the deck.

I have never seen an eagle fly that close before. It was almost touching the house! God sent the eagle that day so my daughter and pastor would see the fulfillment of my request as well. Otherwise, I'm sure no one would have believed me. I now know for certain that HEAVEN IS REAL, and my husband had indeed arrived safely!

The next week I attended a concert by the Gospelaires at a local country church. The first song they sang was about sailing into heaven on a sailboat. I believe God sent that song for me, to help me heal. I cried, grieving, and rejoicing at the same time. We had always enjoyed sailing together. Part of dealing with my grief was designing our headstone. It was inspired by that song. It features the hand of God reaching down out of the clouds, welcoming our sailboat with an eagle flying overhead.

Written on it is John 3:16 NOW ENJOYING ETERNAL LIFE WITH JESUS.

I did wonder why God took my husband so young, especially since we had just started to do mission trips. We had recently done two trips with our pastor and friends. I chose instead, to thank God every day for the 25 years we had together.

Focusing on the positive instead of the negative helped me through this time.

Since then, God has given me the opportunity to do many mission trips as far away as Guatemala, Cuba and Sierra Leone, Africa. God continues to be my Rock and Shield to this day. I could not even imagine going through this time in my life without Him!

1 Those who live in the shelter of the Most High
will find rest in the shadow of the Almighty.
2 This I declare about the Lord:
He alone is my refuge, my place of safety;
He is my God, and I trust him.
3 For He will rescue you from every trap
and protect you from deadly disease.
4 He will cover you with his feathers.
He will shelter you with his wings.
His faithful promises are your armor and protection.
5 Do not be afraid of the terrors of the night,
nor the arrow that flies in the day.
6 Do not dread the disease that stalks in darkness,
nor the disaster that strikes at midday.
7 Though a thousand fall at your side,
though ten thousand are dying around you,
these evils will not touch you.
8 Just open your eyes,
and see how the wicked are punished.
9 If you make the Lord your refuge,
if you make the Most High your shelter,
10 no evil will conquer you;
no plague will come near your home.
11 For he will order his angels
to protect you wherever you go.
12 They will hold you up with their hands
so you won't even hurt your foot on a stone.
13 You will trample upon lions and cobras;
you will crush fierce lions and serpents under your feet!
14 The Lord says, "I will rescue those who love me.
I will protect those who trust in my name.
15 When they call on me, I will answer;
I will be with them in trouble. I will rescue and honor them.
16 I will reward them with a long life
and give them my salvation."

Psalm 91 (NLT)

My husband was Gordon William Aitken, Apr 5, 1951—Feb 5, 1996.

I feel our daughter Cyndi has been dealing with the loss of her father for many years and even today she feels his presence in her home watching over her.

As far as I know our son Greg never talked about it. However, after sharing about my request of his dad and God answering by sending the eagle, he had a huge eagle tattooed on his shoulder with its wings outspread, wrapping around his shoulder. I feel this was a healing process for him.

I don't believe my mother-in-law ever got over the loss of her son.

I have shared many parts of my journey verbally over the past 27 years. Several times I've shared my experiences of feeling his spirit leave his body and watch me as well as how God sent us the eagle, with friends during their last days. I've shared this with them, hoping to give them peace and hope. This is the first time I have written my story down. I hope that it will bring comfort, peace and hope to others dealing with grief.

Author Bio: Diana [Aitken] Manuel
God has been with Diana through the years and continues to guide her footsteps every day. She was very fortunate to find love again and has been happily married for 21 years now.

Ritchie, NB

Finding Grief

Written as told by Luke Budreau

Luke and Vanessa met at bible college. Their relationship started as a long-distance relationship with Luke living in the USA and Vanessa in Canada.

Vanessa was in a serious car accident and broke her femur. Hospital time and recovery took months, which expedited their relationship as Luke took on the role of caregiver. The following summer they were engaged. The summer after that they were married.

They both knew they wanted to have children. It was one of Luke's life goals to have children; to be a father. They didn't wait very long before trying to get pregnant. Luke loved kids and loved working with kids.

One morning in their tiny apartment, Luke was laying on the mattress on the floor without a bedframe. It was a windowless room and pitch black. Vanessa turned on the ceiling light and walked into the room. She gave Luke a pine box.

Inside the box was a positive pregnancy test. They were elated that it was so easy to see their dreams come true. The next few weeks the enormity of their situation settled on them as they realized Vanessa was a Canadian, living in the USA, without health coverage and about to have a baby. She was still under her student healthcare which would run out in two months.

The month after she received her green card, she forfeited it and they decided to move to Canada. It took Luke a year-and-a-half to be able to immigrate to Canada, which left them living apart again.

Since Vanessa has a complex heart condition, they were connected with a specialist. The doctor closely followed the pregnancy. Very early in the pregnancy there were some genetic markers for differences. At the 12 week scan it wasn't shocking to see these differences, given the depth and complexity of Vanessa's condition. They were prepared that some may be passed on genetically.

At the 14-week scan they noticed some differences in the heart and the bowel. At that time, they talked about getting the IWK in Halifax involved. The doctors tried to make Luke and Vanessa realize that this was very serious, however Luke and Vanessa didn't even consider the possibility of this situation becoming as serious as it was.

At about 22 week they had a scan at the IWK which provided them with the information they needed about the baby's valves and heart condition so they could make a plan of action. These words reinforced Luke and Vanessa's hopes that this wasn't serious and would be fixed by medication and surgeries, even in utero. They nervously went to the appointment with hope that they would find answers.

Luke and Vanessa shared their situation with their friends and family, requesting prayer. Luke remembers the nurse saying, "Oh look! She's curled up." Then the nurse got very quiet. She set the wand down and left the room.

Both Luke and Vanessa immediately realized something was seriously wrong. Vanessa told Luke she thought they'd lost the baby. The obstetrician came back into the room and gave them the sad news that the baby had died at some point during the last week.

Before leaving Halifax, on a January day they had to go through the process of labor and delivery of the still birth. At 23 weeks gestation, they named her Nevaeh Hope, Nevaeh being "heaven" spelled backwards. The process was about 13 hours long.

Their pastor, Matthew Maxwell's birthday was that day and he willingly dropped everything to be with them during this difficult process. Their family were also with them. They felt serene and peaceful. It was a special moment for Vanessa because that was the moment, she became a mother. She was full of grief and love at the same time.

They both were in a state of shock as they had fully expected everything was going to be okay. Both Luke and Vanessa felt they went into a dark place, grieving the loss of Nevaeh. They continued to live apart for another year and three months, which also contributed to their grief.

Vanessa was processing her grief at "home" while talking to Luke on the phone where he lived in the USA. While Vanessa kind of "sat" in her grief, Luke was living a pseudo-bachelor life, ignoring his emotions.

When Luke was in Grade 4 he discovered his name meant "Bringer of light". He was always the humorous guy who brings positivity to everyone. He now took the role of the one Vanessa could lean on and always be positive when she needed encouragement.

Over the next three years, while enduring four miscarriages, Luke continued to hold the role of encourager. Vanessa had a difficult time dealing with her identity; was she a mother? She didn't have children, but she had given birth to a child. She had to deal with a lot of doubts about if they would ever have a family.

Luke often said, "We just need to give it more time. It's going to happen." While Luke felt very positive, Vanessa felt hopeless but very driven to get that dream they'd always wanted.

Vanessa began to feel anger and resentment at herself, at the situation and at God who would allow this to happen. While she worked through her stages of grief, Luke continued to be positive, and not really allowing himself to feel his grief.

In 2019 they got pregnant. There were some small markers but nothing significant. Because of Vanessa's heart condition, they delivered their baby at IWK.

They stayed at IWK for a month before the birth. It was a traumatizing but beautiful natural birth. They named their daughter Eleanora.

Other than the cord being wrapped around her neck twice, everything seemed to be normal. Suddenly, all that loss and grief was gone. For Luke, he continued to ignore his grief, as if it didn't happen. For Vanessa, her dream of having a daughter had finally come true. She was elated!

They were in the NICU for about a week. They were waiting on a cardiac scan so they could go home. They were so grateful for the Ronald McDonald House, but they were ready to go home.

When they finally received the results, it indicated there were some issues that would need further investigation, but they could go home and return for more tests later. That April, they enjoyed the first few weeks of being new parents.

That year both their families experienced a lot of loss. Vanessa's maternal grandmother passed away. Luke lost his great uncle, then his uncle died in a tragic motorcycle accident. A week after his uncle died Luke's grandfather also passed away. This all happened between June and August. During this time Luke was still living in the USA during the week and coming home to Canada on weekends.

It was a weird time for them because Eleanora was such a beautiful bright light in their lives, and they were grieving their losses at the same time. Eleanora's name also means "light". They spent a lot of time with their family that summer.

At the end of the summer Eleanora had more tests done in Halifax. They discovered she has Pulminary Vein Stenosis (PVS). The doctor explained it many times, trying to get them to understand the seriousness of the situation. They did research and discovered it is a terminal disease with no cure.

That brought on a whole new chapter of "living grief". Vanessa felt that she'd lost her dream that had finally come true. The next three years were spent undergoing continuous tests and scans to monitor Eleanora's condition.

In 2021, the scans were negative. The physical nature of some of the veins changed and they were almost completely closed off. At that point, Luke finally encountered the gravity of his daughter's fatality, not knowing how much longer she would live. Until then, he had blind optimism, thinking it was just a birth defect and will probably get better. *It's probably not even PVS,* he thought. Finally, the truth about the situation was clear to him.

With that came the grief of Nevaeh's death as well as his many family members' deaths. At that point Luke finally started to mourn. During the next three months Luke was able to lament his heart to God as he stepped out of the shock and reality dawned on him. God was able to hear the real cry of his heart.

Luke felt complete desolation. He finally realized what Vanessa had been going through, basically on her own because he wasn't going through it with her. Emotions such as anger, rage and doubt came pouring through. Depression and loneliness tried to engulf him. He wanted to isolate. Luke is so grateful for the communities that surrounded him as they pulled him through that tragic time. He experienced physical symptoms of tiredness and lack of motivation.

In February of 2021 they had their second daughter, Miller Elaine, who they affectionately call "Millie". Even during the early days of Millie's life, Luke found himself focused on Eleanora's health. He would cradle Eleanora, pressing his forehead against her forehead, completely engulfed in affection and concern for her.

He latched onto everything that Eleanora was, at the expense of his wife and second daughter, Millie.

It was a painful process for Luke, and he worked through it. Hope looked different at that point. It wasn't ignoring the loss. It was acknowledging the loss at the same time as realizing God is still good and Eleanora is still a miracle. Luke realized Eleanora had made a difference... she had already made an impact on the community around her.

She has given them something that nobody else could. He was able to admit to Vanessa that he wasn't okay. Together they realized Eleanora was not okay either.

During that time, God provided a lot of healing and reconciliation to their family. He's also given them a new kind of hope, being surrounded in prayer.

The scans that were done in June 2022 showed that the veins were better. The doctor said, "I shouldn't say this, but the veins have opened up more."

Luke referred to an Old Testament story of Shadrach, Meshack and Abednego. The three men were about to be thrown into a furnace of fire because they wouldn't worship idols. They said, "*even if* our God doesn't save us, we won't bow down."

"Even if" became Luke and Vanessa's mantra. They realized God is good and even if the worst thing happens, they know God is good and they have been blessed to have Eleanora in their lives. The grief they have now is an ongoing grief because Eleanora's life is a daily miracle.

A large part of Luke's healing was to work through forgiving himself for not grieving with his wife, years ago. He had to give himself the space he needed to grieve.

When asked if he could travel back in time and say something to his younger self, Luke said he would say, "Grieve! Allow yourself to grieve."

He had worked in the mental health industry for five years and had all the coping tools needed to grieve, but he didn't allow himself to use them and grieve. He said it was like he had blinders on.

"Optimism without doubt and grief and a possible negative outcome," Luke said, "is almost just ignorance. Whereas optimism *in spite* of the doubt and grief is kind of what faith is. Faith is a hope in something we can't see."

As an eternal optimist it is sometimes difficult to accept reality when it doesn't fall within our optimistic bubble. Luke cautions professionals who know the tools of grief to actually use them on themselves when they're in the midst of grief.

He also said, "Being able to see a positive outlook is a way to persevere through the situation instead of 'in spite of' the situation."

I asked Luke what he would want readers who are grieving to know. He said, "Never stop talking about the grief." He added, "Don't let people tell you it is wrong to talk about your grief."

Luke encourages readers to share their grief with others. The most powerful thing he experienced was the support of the community, they received when they shared their grief with others. Shortly after Eleanora was diagnosed with PVS, they found a small on-line community of people who have/ had children with PVS.

Some of them have adult children who have survived PVS, and some have a child who has passed away. This community really helped them when they needed it the most.

Author Bio: Luke & Vanessa Budreau

Luke Budreau and his wife Vanessa are a loving couple residing in Canada with their two beautiful daughters and two happy dogs. Luke and Vanessa have been happily married since 2014, and they have been living in New Brunswick for the past seven years. Together, Luke and Vanessa make a perfect team, balancing each other out in every aspect of their lives. They are both devoted parents who work hard to provide for their children. They enjoy spending time with their family and exploring the natural beauty of the great outdoors.

A Mother's Wish

Written by Thanh Campbell, Orphan 32

My family left Ontario to move to New Brunswick in 1981. It was a hard transition, leaving family and friends. Even though we lived in the countryside just outside of Cambridge, Ontario, we had the best of both worlds — city life and rural retreat. I didn't know what to expect moving to the Maritimes. It didn't help that my brother David said that all there is to do in the Maritimes was to be a woodsman or a fisherman. I envisioned us living in a shack in the woods and having to walk to the village to get on our fishing boat. Needless to say, I suffered through the long trip in our family station wagon from Cambridge to Moncton thinking about how I was going to grow up to become a lumberjack.

Arriving in Moncton, we discovered it was a very urban area. We lived in a suburb called Riverview, and while my brothers went to middle school in the city, I finished elementary school at Lower Coverdale Elementary School. It was a small country school with a wonderful, welcoming community feel to it, very much like my former school, Cambridge Christian School, in Ontario.

In Grade Seven I transitioned to Riverview Junior High School, which was a bigger urban school. Then I graduated to an even bigger Riverview High School with over a thousand students. Even though I got involved with school activities like band and the track-and-field team, I felt lost and very much alone. My insecurities got the best of me, and I found myself caught up in trying to fit in with my peers, while at the same time trying to present myself as a respectable pastor's kid.

Throughout my high school years, I felt I was on a mission to try and figure out who I really was. Not who I thought I wanted to be, or what others thought of me, but who I really was. Although most teens deal with this as part of the self-actualization process, I felt for me it was different. For the most part, my peers knew their parents, they knew where they were born, and they knew their medical history. Being adopted, I had no connection to my heritage as they did. The only resource I had at my disposal to guide me was the way I felt according to each experience; I had to "trust" my feelings.

Even though I was brought up in a religious home, I did not fully grasp the understanding of a God that would interact with me. Instead, I had a more distant connection and viewed Him more as a judge who sat up "on high" and who was waiting for me to mess up. I did not put my trust in Him, rather I feared Him and what He thought of me, whoever "I" was. I did not trust anyone else with my deepest feelings, especially about my adoption. I felt somewhat like a ticking time bomb with my real feelings being suppressed. I felt very alone in this great big world. At the same time, however, I was very good at keeping a very amicable exterior, but inside me a great battle was being waged.

I developed a trust issue — trust in myself. Sometimes I would think or do things that I knew deep down were not right, but I would do them anyway. It was like I couldn't even live up to the moral code I had set for myself. For the most part, I was left trusting my gut feeling, even though I knew how feelings could be. It was like an internal checklist that I would score myself upon. Learning about who I was and what I liked would come down to how I felt about things. *What else did I have to go on?*

This inner conflict caused me a lot of grief and moved me to do a lot of introspection. I was awkwardly making my way through adolescence while still trying to understand what this void was in my life. When I was thirteen years old, I was going through my photo albums and personal files my mother had collected for me over the years — mementos, elementary school class pictures, etc. On one of her trips home, my sister, Joan, handed me a package of information with some pictures in it. As I sorted through the package there were documents about Vietnam, a short story written by her, titled *Five O'clock Follies* and a letter from the government signed by a lady named Victoria Leach. There was also an adoption certificate and two copies of a birth certificate — one in Vietnamese and one in English.

As I looked at the different names and places on the birth certificate, I thought about the hospital where was born. It was in a place called Phuoc Tuy. I looked at a globe — these were the days before the Internet — but it was not there. Next, I found an atlas and looked at a map of Vietnam. I found Saigon (now called Ho Chi Minh City) and started scanning around the map for Phuoc Tuy. But nothing close to that name was near Saigon. I went to the outlying areas, and I found it!

Phuoc Tuy is a province east of Saigon, in a region called Ba Ria/Vung Tau on the South China Sea. Even though it was just some place on a map, I was very excited to locate the place where I was born. Excitement turned to curiosity, and I started to wonder how I had ended up in an orphanage in Saigon if the hospital where I was born was 100 kilometres away. I had heard stories of how kids were left at the doorstep of churches and orphanages, others were found in burned out villages, and some even left to die by the side of the road. Surely, I was not one of those kids; I had identification papers. So how then, had I ended up at an orphanage in Saigon?

I asked my mom, "Having been born way over here" — pointing to a place on the map — "how did I end up there?" – pointing to Saigon. Searching for the right words, she said, "Thanh, it is time that you know that these papers are most likely not your own . . ." My immediate reaction was of shock and bewilderment.

How could this be? They had always called me Thanh, which matched the name on these papers and everything else that came with me when I was adopted. She then shared with me the information that Victoria Leach had given them when I first arrived. The fact was, just because papers were associated with an orphan when they arrived in Canada, it did not necessarily mean they belonged to that child. In order to be allowed to leave the country, official government documents — either a birth certificate or some type of identification papers — had to accompany each child, even if they weren't really a match. We have come to find out that some of the papers were from children that had died - others may have even belonged to a child that was left behind in the orphanage.

"You mean my name isn't really Thanh?" I asked.

"You'll always be Thanh to us and that's all that matters, right?" my mom quickly tried to reassure me.

I knew what she meant, and that she meant well, but something did not sit right with me after that. My heart sank and my mind started to whirl. My thoughts started to spin in my head: *A name is how human beings are identified, if you don't have a name, how do you exist? It's like being called Baby X.* I was nameless. I had no real identification. I felt like a lost soul, wandering around trying to find something solid to possess. *If I was not Thanh, then who was I?* That was the only way people had ever known me. I was the kid with the cute dimples and unique name, hard to pronounce, but once you got it, it was hard to forget.

I had spent so much time explaining to others how to pronounce my name, and now it wasn't even mine. Bizarre thoughts plagued me: *What if I get to heaven and I meet the real Thanh, would he be angry I was using his name all this time?*

Though this was the start of an identity crisis, I was thirteen and I was able to put it aside and get distracted in other areas of my teen angst. But somewhere in the back of my mind finding out my real name plagued me. I wanted to get to the bottom of it.

What's in a Name?
That summer, I got to travel alone to Scotland to visit my sister Nancy and her husband, Jack, who was studying at the University of Glasgow. We had an amazing experience during those three weeks. One of the most important moments for me was visiting Inverary Castle, the ancestral home of the Campbell clan. Even though I did not have the

Campbell bloodline in me, I felt as much like a Campbell as anyone else with the last name; so, I signed the Family Guest Book. I am sure it was a funny scene seeing a Vietnamese guy signing a Scottish family registrar; but at that point, I was starting to understand that family membership goes beyond shared genes.

Later that summer, I had the opportunity to attend Atlantic Pioneer Camp in Prince Edward Island. It was good to get away from the city and the peer pressure I was experiencing. While I was there, I did some further searching in my heart as to the meaning of life . . . and death.

One night after campfire I was moved emotionally by the message, and I was encouraged to say the Sinner's Prayer and accept Jesus into my heart. I was not fully aware of what that meant, even though I had grown up in the Church. To be honest, it was not that I was putting my trust in God; for me, it was the decision that I did not want to go to hell forever. If that's what it took to seal the deal, I wanted to make sure I was on the right side. At camp I had made the decision to be a Christ follower, not for its rewards, but more not wanting to experience the alternative.

After summer, school started and the same patterns in life seem to emerge. My trust in people deteriorated even more. It was like *The Great Sadness* described in Wm. Paul Young's book *The Shack*. Like a shroud that was quickly enfolding me or dark waters that never let me surface no matter how much I tried to fight to keep my head above water.

I remember lying on my bed asking God to take me away from this world of loneliness. I was consumed with the thought that no one will ever "get me." *If they really knew who I was, they wouldn't do things that would betray me or hurt my feelings.* I didn't just want God to take away the feeling of being empty or lost, I wanted Him to take me away, to leave this life and be in Heaven if it meant no more pain and no more sorrow. When I woke the next morning, I was angry at God for my unanswered prayer. The question burned in me: *Why am I still here?*

At that moment, I received an immediate answer that spoke to my heart, "**I love you. You are my son. I have a purpose for you, and I am not finished with you yet.**"

It was a very powerful message to a child that was struggling with some deep abandonment and attachment issues. I was not feeling fully accepted by the world, not feeling like there was a purpose to life, or that there was a real hope for a fulfilling future. It was a dark world to live in at that young age. These divine words of comfort came as a soothing balm to a hurting soul; a message that would bear repeating at a later stage in life. Having God state His fatherhood to me was a hard concept for me to grasp. How can I be his son? I thought Jesus was his son. I was familiar enough with the Bible to know that was true. I was adopted into the Campbell family, sharing only their last name, but knowing beyond a shadow of a doubt that I belonged to them.

Here I was, in a moment of desperation and I received affirmation from my heavenly Father, ensuring me of my adoption into His spiritual family, the Family of God. (John 1:12, NIV) *"Yet to all who did receive Him, to those who believed in His name, He gave the right to become children of God."* Many years later this message would bear repeating, but under very different circumstances.

When My World Turned Upside Down

On October 11, 2001, I was travelling to a meeting in Listowel, Ontario. I was about to pass a sixteen-wheeler on a dark, two-lane highway headed west. The minivan in front of me decided to do the same thing and pulled out in front of me so I had to follow him in order to pass the truck. When the van pulled in front of the truck, it did not leave enough space for my car to get in between. I was now stuck in the eastbound lane with on coming traffic quickly approaching. I veered onto the shoulder of the road but saw some flashing lights with which I was about to collide. Thinking it might be a horse and buggy, since this is Amish country, I swerved back on to the lane. Wanting to avoid the imminent head-on collision, I placed myself in the midst of another one with the on coming eastbound traffic right in front of me.

When I turned the wheel, the rear of my car spun out on the gravel and shot me across the eastbound lane back into the westbound lane. The trucker must have seen this transpiring and slowed down because I was now facing the truck that I had just tried to pass. With the Mack grill bearing down on me, my car continued to spin out of control, and I dropped into an embankment and flipped the vehicle multiple times. The car finally landed at the bottom of the ditch pinned against a tree.

First on the scene were an off-duty firefighter and the head nurse from the Campbell Soup factory just down the road. Although I knew I wasn't physically injured, I was still put through a battery of questions.

The nurse asked, "Sir, how do you feel?"

"Stupid," I replied. They chuckled and breathed a sigh of relief.

I was immediately deemed stable and in my right mind and asked if I could get out of the car. I said, "Yes." But when I undid my seatbelt, I hit the ceiling with a clunk. Still disoriented, I did not realize the car was upside down.

She pleaded with me to get out of the car so I could be assessed. As I crawled out of the window, the kind nurse laid her jacket in the ditch and instructed me to lie still until the paramedics arrived. Still feeling like I was fully functional, I wanted to figure out how I could get to my meeting on time. This was not to be, for when paramedics arrived, they strapped me to the spinal board and hauled me out of that muddy pit; shaking their heads in amazement that I had survived the crash.

I was told I was lucky to be alive at least ten times enroute to the Listowel hospital. It was also mentioned repeatedly by the nurse during the initial triage intake and the on-duty police officer who came to visit me a couple of hours later to take the accident report. The words "*being lucky*" played over and over like a chorus, but never really struck a chord with me. It was not until a nurse said as I was being placed in a waiting area, "Young man, you have an angel looking over you, maybe more than one. From what they tell me, you should be dead, a hundred feet from your car, but you're not and there is a reason for that . . . I don't know what it is, but there's a reason."

I was wheeled into a darkened room to wait for the doctor to assess me for spinal injury. It was very uncomfortable being strapped to the board. I was forced to stare up at the florescent lights. Every time I closed my eyes, I would see the chrome grill coming at me. I started searching my mind and thinking of what could have been. Questions plagued me. *Why was I still here? Why was I not lying a hundred feet from my car, in the ditch with a white cloth over me?* It was a sobering question and one that I wanted answered.

In that moment, I heard a still small voice say, **"I love you Thanh, you are my son and I have a purpose for you, and I am not done with you yet."** It was like an echo from the past. I vaguely remembered hearing that before, strangely familiar, yet with a different overtone. It brought a sense of peace to me, and I was able to rest there forgetting the discomfort I could not escape before.

A couple of weeks earlier, I had been wrestling with some spiritual issues and I had renewed my vows to God. Somehow this experience assured me that I was being protected and that those vows were being taken seriously.

A couple of hours later, I walked out of that hospital a different person from the one who had been wheeled in many hours earlier.

In 1986, after my mom told me about my birth papers, I grew up assuming I would never find my parents. I knew they existed and something inside of me told me they were still alive, but I never considered the possibility that there would be a family looking for me.

In the movie, *An American Tale,* a little mouse named Fievel comes to America from Russia and is separated from his family during a storm at sea. His sister Tanya still believes that Fievel survived and is in America with them. At one point in the movie, the two are looking up at the starry night sky from their respective places of being "lost" and singing the song "Somewhere Out There".

I was thirteen when I went with my sister and her daughter Rebecca to see that movie. I never knew at that time how profoundly that song would affect me. Still today when I play the song, a void causes me to cry out. There is something deep seated in me that triggers a great sadness about being separated from my family; one that I suppress and do not let surface very often. Specifically, my sadness is losing a mother I never got to meet. Like in the movie, I imagined her looking up at the stars at night wondering where in the world I was and praying that she would find me.

In 2009, I was on another trip-of-a-lifetime, and I flew back to meet a family I never knew existed. Three years earlier the whole story of my journey to Canada became household news and was featured in mainstream media across the globe. Through the media, a family read about me in their local newspaper in Saigon (now Ho Chi Minh City). The journalist who wrote the article, helped them to track me down.

After some emails back and forth, we finally concluded that we would have to do a DNA test to prove any type of connection. (No, I didn't go on Maury) The test results came back a 99.999% match. I had found my birth father after 30 years. So, we knew we had to call and share the news with him.

I called my friend and translator, Khanh and told him the news of the results. He was very pleased for he had called the Nguyen family before we did the paternity test to ask, quite frankly, what their intentions were in making contact with me. Mr. Nguyen stated very clearly that his intentions were honest, and he just wanted to know if I was his son and to know that I was happy in life.

We arranged a time to place a call to the family in Vietnam. I was excited and nervous - *how was my life going to change? What will they be like? Will the language barrier hinder our ability to express what we want to say?* I was afraid that first impressions over the phone wouldn't be the same as it would be if we met in person.

I had my friend Jason Pluim film the event, just in case we needed to use the footage later. I invited my dad and Trent and his girlfriend Lia

Pouli to be there (two of the orphans that flew with me in 1975). Khanh placed the call and we waited for them to pick up the line on the other end. It felt like an eternity, but eventually someone answered. It was an older man's voice, and he was speaking Vietnamese.

Khanh explained that it was my father on the line. He shared the news about the results of the paternity test, and it went silent on the end of line. Then, speaking very quickly, Mr. Nguyen spoke with Khanh, telling him how happy he was to receive this news. His son Thao had received the same news as us a couple of days earlier but did not tell his dad of the results. He wanted to wait for us to tell him on the phone. You could hear them laughing about how hard it was for him to keep the secret waiting for our phone call. He was glad he didn't have to keep it in anymore.

Nearly speechless, I stammered my introduction and explained who the people in the room with me were. I reiterated that we had got the positive results and how pleased, yet perplexed, I was to be introducing myself for the first time over the phone. Khanh relayed the message and then entered into a lengthy conversation with my birth father. After a while, Khanh paused their conversation and translated what my father had said, "He is very happy today to receive the news.

He's very touched that he found out that you are his son, that he has been looking for the last thirty-one years . . . and unfortunately that . . ." — I could see Khanh struggling with his own emotions — ". . . your (birth) mom passed away, and just before she passed, she told him 'Whatever it takes, go find him' and he's sorry your [birth] mom is not around to see the results today." My dad, Reverend William, spoke up then so my birth father could hear. "I am sorry my wife isn't here also . . ."

Then Mr. Nguyen shared his condolences with my dad. This was so surreal for me to hear this. Here I was sitting in my living room with my two dads talking about my two moms, consoling each other, and creating a bond between them. I tried to imagine my mom sitting there beside my dad with her legs crossed at the ankles, beaming at what was taking place. I wondered what my birth mother had been like and what she would be saying now if she were there.

My father expressed how grateful he was to the Campbells for taking care of me. My dad replied that it was their pleasure and that I was a very easy child to raise. Khanh continued to translate my father's words. "What had happened to you was out of his wish. He did not want to give you away whatsoever; he has lost his blood and he is very sorry about that."

My father's side of the story was told to us. Mr. Nguyen was a high-ranking general in the South Vietnamese army and was working with the Americans. His wife, Nguyen Ngoc Thu, was so beautiful that the American G.I.s wanted her to work directly for them on the base. The Nguyens used a local Catholic orphanage as a boarding school for their children as it had a good reputation for the quality of care and education they provided. (There is a chance the other Vietnamese military personnel were doing the same with their children and that what happened to me might have happened to other children that were evacuated. There could be other parents who have the opportunity to be reunited with their son or daughter.)

Periodically the Nguyens went to the orphanage to visit their two boys and then returned to their post. After I was born, I stayed with my parents for a year before being placed in the orphanage with my siblings.

As the war intensified in April 1975, my parents were not able to visit as often. One day in early April, American soldiers came to take children away from the orphanage as part of Operation Babylift evacuation. Most of the children were being sent to Saigon, with their destination being the various countries that had responded to the pleas for help. We don't know if this was prearranged by the nuns, but they had a sense of who should go and what children needed to stay.

Just when it seemed they were done, one soldier came back and took a baby from the arms of one of the Sisters. She pleaded with the soldiers not to take him and tried to explain that he was not an orphan.

But the soldier either did not understand what she was saying, or he did not care. As he carried the baby boy off to the waiting military Jeep, two brothers followed, caressing his head, and holding his tiny hands in theirs, trying to keep him calm. They knew something the soldier did not, that their little brother had severe breathing problems and if he got too upset by crying, he would stop breathing and pass out.

The brothers were successful in keeping the child calm. A quick-thinking Sister ran and got some official papers and pinned them to the child's birth bracelet. The infant was passed to another soldier waiting in the back of the Jeep. As the jeep pulled away down the road, the brothers stood there with their caregivers, bewildered at what had just happened to their baby brother. Where were those soldiers taking him? Was he going to the hospital? Would he be coming back later? And why were the nuns so upset? They did not know that when they let go of my hand, it would be the last time they saw their little brother for 34 years.

A New Path
I ended up at the Go Vap Orphanage in Saigon. How many other institutions in which I stayed enroute to Go Vap is still in question. At the Go Vap Orphanage I was baptized and given a new Catholic name, Nguyen Phaolo Thanh. I was named "Phaolo" after the Apostle Paul. Yet they still left my original birth bracelet on me and kept my birth papers on file.

On April 30, 1975, when Saigon fell to the Communist Regime, the war came to an end. Having lost the war and with the American troops pulling out of the city, South Vietnamese officers quickly scrambled to reclaim their children from the orphanages and plan their own escape route. For many South Vietnamese soldiers, these plans failed. The Nguyens were no exception.

When they returned to the orphanage, my parents were met with the horrific story of their baby being taken. Minh Thanh and Ngoc Thu's hearts broke, as any parents would. Panic stricken over their missing baby, questions of how and why, came flooding down upon them. My birth mother collapsed in grief. *Where could they have gone?*

Reclaiming their other two boys, Thuan and Thien, they left as a broken family, trying to comfort each other from an irreversible pain that would linger for decades.

The Mission

Immediately after leaving the orphanage in Ba Ria with their family, Minh Thanh and Ngoc Thu started on their quest to find their missing son, stopping at other orphanages, and hearing the same story of American soldiers coming to take children to the city. When asked where the soldiers were taking the children, the orphanages replied, "to America."

Soon after, Minh Thanh was captured by the Communists and placed in a re-education camp as a prisoner of war. His downtrodden wife was left to fend for herself and her two boys. After two years, Minh Thanh was released. The family was relocated to the border of Cambodia and Vietnam. This was a strategic move by the Communist government so that if foreign invading armies came, there was a border community that would act as a stop gap before they could infiltrate the interior.

The family was forced to survive off the land and anything they could scrounge to make shelter and find to eat. Their son Minh Thao was born at this time, which added to the desperation of their situation. It was many years before it was safe for them to return to Saigon, which had since been renamed Ho Chi Minh City. It was named after the North Vietnamese dictator.

They settled in the city and started rebuilding their life. They established a convenience store that served food and drinks. Their second eldest son, Thien, eventually took over the business and it continues to be run by his family today. The eldest, Thuan, went into the construction business and continues to work in this field.

The youngest son, Thao, went to school and eventually moved on to study at college and university. He held a prominent position with the city's hydro company before moving on to work for the Intel Corporation making microchips for computers.

While they were living off the land in the jungle between Vietnam and Cambodia, Mrs. Nguyen was attacked by disease stemming from the chemical residue from Agent Orange and Napalm used during the conflict; now seeping into the local watershed. She developed pancreatic cancer and in 1987, after only a short time in the city, she died. Mr. Nguyen remembers her last moments. His beloved wife, Ngoc Thu, looked up at him and pulled him close to deliver her final wish. "Keep looking for our baby, keep looking for our little Thanh, never give up, never give up . . ." Weeping, he held her and promised he would never quit looking for their lost son, Nguyen Ngoc Minh Thanh. Her sons say that their mom did not die of pancreatic cancer, but of a broken heart over her lost baby boy.

Although Minh Thanh eventually remarried, he kept his promise to his first wife. One day in 2005 he caught wind of a news article about Vietnamese American adoptees that were coming back to see their homeland. They were going to be staying at hotel in Ho Chi Minh City. *This could be his chance to get more information, maybe even meet his long-lost son*, he thought. But instead of the help he hoped to get, Mr. Nguyen was stonewalled and denied access to the Ameri-Asian cohort. It was almost as wrenching as the first time he lost his baby, to come so close and then be sidelined.

Would he ever find his son? He believed there was a God out there that knew where his son was, but wondered if his son Ngoc Minh Thanh knew that he had a family that longed to see him? Did he know that he had had a mother who died of a broken heart and brothers who lived with the guilt of letting him go with those soldiers? It seemed a very distant possibility that they would ever find him...until he read that news article and God told him in his dream that the article was about me, his long-lost son, his Baby Thanh.

The Picture That Took My Breath Away
After two years of fundraising, we were able to fly as a family back to Vietnam and reunite in Saigon. One night my father arrived at the hotel and had a small envelope for me. I opened it and inside there were two black-and-white photos that my father had made prints of for me. One photo was of my father and another one of my mother, taken when

144

they were both young. He was dressed sharp, and I could see some similar physical traits to me. She was breathtakingly beautiful. It looked like she could have been a Hollywood star; from the way her hair was done to the tilt of her chin. These pictures were professionally done. It was the first time I had seen an image of her, and I was moved with a sense of regret of not having had the chance to know her. Tears welling up, I wanted to tell her that I was back home and that she could rest in peace. Instead, I stood there in silence and said a prayer of thanks for a mother I never knew.

The next day my father took us out to visit my mother's gravesite. I wasn't sure what to think, feel, or expect. *This was how I would meet my mother?* It was obvious the pain of losing her was still poignant, as he feebly knelt down and spoke to her; sharing the news that their son had been found and was standing over her with his young family — their grandchildren. It was touching to see all that he was feeling. It had been a long time since she left him with this mission to find me and here, I was standing beside him. It was a bitter-sweet end to a lifelong mission.

As I stood staring at the picture of her on the tombstone, I thought of my adoptive mom. I miss my times with her, drinking tea and talking about my day. I wondered what rituals I would have had with my birth mother. *Would she like who I was as a person? Would we have the type of relationship I had had with mom?* At that moment I felt no connection, no deep sadness for losing her from my life. When I stand in front of my mom's grave in Kirkwall, Ontario, I am flooded with memories and feelings of love and being loved. I felt more sorrow for my father, who had held on to the quest to find me. I am no expert in the afterlife, but for a moment, I envisioned my two moms meeting in heaven; having given them both a lot to talk about. No doubt it would be a long conversation.

Author Bio: Thanh Campbell, Orphan 32

Mr. Campbell lives in Drayton ON. He and his wife Teresa have a combined family of 6 kids and 1 crazy dog, Theo.

He is a professional speaker and Canadian Best-Selling Author. He has toured across Canada and spoken internationally sharing his story. He has had the privilege to speak for the United Nations in Toronto, multiple school boards and Fortune 500 companies across Canada.

In 2014, Mr. Campbell was awarded the distinguished **Paul Harris Fellow Award,** a prestigious award presented by the Rotary for those whose efforts are commended in community building. He is a licensed minister with Anchor Ministerial which is based in Fergus.

Most recently Thanh was appointed as the Canadian Director of Partners Worldwide Canada. He has been asked to sit on a number of boards and committees including the MacKids Fundraising Committee, the Hamilton Media Advisory Council, which discusses the issue of diversity and multiculturalism portrayed in the media and Promise Keepers/Impactus Canada Advisory Board.

Thanh was born in Vietnam and came to Canada as part of the last flight out of Saigon in 1975 with 56 other orphan children. Their story was captured numerous times in the media including the Toronto Star, the Hamilton Spectator, Ottawa Citizen, Vancouver Sun, Saigon Newspaper, and included in the French Consulate Newsletter. He has been invited to be a guest on such programs as CBC Radio, TVO, Canada AM, 100 Huntley Street.

Thanh has written his memoir titled Orphan 32 and most recently his illustrated children's book, Lost and Found - Orphan 32 Goes Home. Www.Orphan32.com

My Journey With Grief

Written by Susan Hood

Hi. My name is Susan Hood. I was asked by Tammy to share my grief story.

Grief is something that can be hard to share. It's how we deal with grief that is important. We are all made differently in God's eyes. Our wonderful, beautiful Creator wanted it that way.

For me, dealing with grief has made me stronger over the years.

I lost my dad in 1998. Ten years later, I lost my sister (the youngest of our family) at the young age of 36.

My dad died of suicide while my mom was away in Florida. The hardest thing I had to do was to tell my mom and the rest of the family that dad had died.

I've had years of sadness beyond words. Grief had set in to cause me to be bitter. Why? I still ask that question. Every day I wonder. I may never know the answer! That was the beginning of my journey through grief. Our world is changed by grief; it is too hard to understand.

My dad and I were very close. We cried, talked, laughed, and shared stories. Dad never showed his struggles or talked about his difficult times. Grief can cause us struggles, difficult times, and pain.

I miss the times we went to town shopping and just spending time together. Dad never talked about the things hurting him like I do. I just listened. "You are a good listener," Dad told me. Sometimes people share their grief to those who can listen and understand.

Then there was my little sister who died and had four young children. My sisters were in Woodstock shopping. My youngest sister was the passenger while my other sister was driving. I was home taking care of three of the children - her two oldest girls, and my young child.

I received a phone call from the R.C.M.P. that there had been a serious car accident. My sister that was driving was bruised and hurt. My youngest sister was transported to Moncton hospital. She had severe head trauma. The doctors described it as shaken baby syndrome.

I spent 4 1/2 weeks at The Moncton Hospital while my sister was there. She had numerous surgeries. I cried, prayed and talked to her. I was grieving and hurting. I didn't blame God. I also didn't blame my other sister. I held my sister's hands with tears of sadness. It certainly was not easy; grief isn't! As I watched her, I realized God was in control. I would say that over and over, not questioning why or blaming anyone. I simply left it in the Master's hands.

After being in the Fredericton hospital for four years she passed away. I remember getting that call from a nurse who said my sister had gone peacefully. She never recovered and I knew she wasn't going to get better.

The doctors indicated she was not able to talk or realize things in life. I still believe she knew us. When we talked to her, she blinked her eyes - at us - as we asked her things. My sister wouldn't want to live her life the way she was.

However, leaving behind four young children was enough grief to ask why? My life changed that day. As years go on and I see her children, my heart aches for them.

In 2021, another grief struck our family. My youngest brother had terminal cancer. This was yet another grief journey, which I was not ready for. One is never ready for grief. After telling us that he was terminally ill, the doctors told him it was something that he may live with for years.

After five years he was in and out of the best cancer hospital in Canada, located in Edmonton, Alberta. He travelled to New Brunswick for our mom's 80th birthday. He told us he wouldn't be able to travel home anymore.

I faithfully prayed and talked to God. Again, I asked "Why?" God knew what He was doing, but I didn't. My brother was in pain until the end of his life.

I talked with him on the phone almost every day. We cried, laughed, and shared memories: both good ones and not so good ones. I was very close to my youngest brother. We talked about life, and how it is not fair sometimes. I talked to him about being strong and positive.

I was grieving and hurting. My heart was broken.

My brother asked me to look after things when he passed. He had a wonderful girlfriend who he loved and adored. He just wanted his suffering to end. I knew what was coming, the painful planning of his arrangements. Our mother suffers with dementia and he knew I needed to take care of things.

I can't imagine what was going through his mind as I told him that I loved him and for him to go peacefully with God. I told him not to worry, I would help look after Mother.

One of the hardest parts was letting go and accepting that my loved one was gone. What helped me through it was praying to God and letting Him be in control of my emotions. I also understood He knew what I was going through and I had to accept His timing.

With my brother, it was difficult that I couldn't be with him for the last days of his life. It was during Covid and it was hard to get flights from New Brunswick to Alberta.

My brother told me he didn't want me to see him like he was, at the end of his life. What really got me through was being able to hear his voice every day when I talked to him on the phone. I realized I couldn't be mad at God because He was in control.

On November 10, 2021, it was a time of sorrow and crying and it was also a joyful time because my brother's suffering was over.

I held a Celebration of Life, which was hard, yet it was also a joy to fulfill his wishes. Grief can be crushing and it can help us to be stronger in life. We realize God is in control all the time.

If I could travel back in time and talk to myself, I would say: "Lord, I know you made me strong for a reason because I wasn't supposed to get this far in life. Because of health issues I wasn't supposed to be able to walk, and I was supposed to be blind." I am able to walk and to see. God had made my brother and I very close. My brother and I talked a lot and he told me, "You have been the strong one in the family, because of your faith."

Looking back at my life, I realize that the grief I went through made me strong.

My advice to those grieving today is to trust God and talk to others who are dealing with grief as well. Be strong, cry when you need to and remember you are not alone!

In conclusion to my grief story the journey of life continues on, as I walk through emotions dealing with my mom's health. As difficult as it is, with family members, each day is a step forward. I'm doing what I feel is the right thing for my mom's best interest. I love my family, even though our view on things in life can cause more grief than we can bear.

I am so thankful for my faith as it helps me when I feel like I can't bear the burden of grief alone. We are never alone with our faith in God. I give God all the glory and praise each day.

Thank you, Tammy for this opportunity. I hope others can find hope, joy, peace and love when going through their journey of grief. I hope my story will help someone deal with grief the way God would want us to. He is the great Healer and will direct our path.

Author Bio: Susan Hood

Susan Hood lives with her husband Jerry in Upper Queensbury, New Brunswick. She is mother to two adopted children. Susan is a loving soul who is always willing to lend a hand. She works as a Personal Support Worker and volunteers at the food bank in Fredericton. She also volunteers at her church, Journey Wesleyan Church in Fredericton. Susan always has a happy smile to encourage her friends, family and even strangers she passes on the street.

Lost Hope

Written by Michael Lock

"You will never amount to anything!"

"You're no good!"

"You should never have been born!"

These were lies attached to my childhood memories. I carried those lies all the way into my early adulthood. Those words taunted me along with feelings of emptiness, anger, rejection, guilt, and shame. This affected me in every area of my life.

I just wanted to be accepted and loved. I wore masks to cover up my pain. I don't mean Halloween masks but invisible masks to cover the ugliness that lived inside me.

When we are children, we are told monsters do not exist. They don't hide inside our closets or under our bed, but they do hide inside of us. I didn't have one monster. I had a whole family of monsters living inside me. They even had names.

They were not something I could dream up, but they were monsters that come from hell. These things came through some really bad experiences I lived through in my own hell.

Hell doesn't torment all at once; it is a very slow torment. The monsters are created by negative words which start off with a tiny little seed spoken over a person. It gets plenty of water and it grows into an ugliness that is not easy to describe. They feed on every negativity and abuse, whether it is physical abuse, verbal abuse, or sexual abuse. Its family works together as a team. They are fear, rejection, and liar. They come with only one purpose. To kill, steal, and destroy, our life. These monsters don't play fair. These are the monsters that lived inside me leading me down a path of destruction.

At the age of 13, I wanted to end my life but I wanted to die in my sleep; to experience some kind of peace, maybe even a bit of joy. One night I was home alone. My parents were out bowling. I went into their bedroom and opened the medicine drawer where they kept prescription pills.

I like blue, so I chose the blue pills to swallow. I went to the kitchen to get a glass of water. I drank down a handful of those blue pills. Not knowing what the outcome was going to be, I waited in the kitchen.

Suddenly, I heard a male voice speaking to me. His voice was right next to me, but no one was there. I couldn't see anyone, but I felt his presence and I felt drawn to him.

He spoke very clearly. He said, "I paid the price at Calvary. My plan for your life is greater than this. I can give you peace and joy. If you call to me and follow me, my plans for you are great!"

I asked, "How do I follow someone I cannot see? Who are you?"

I thought I had gone crazy, or the pills were causing me to hear voices. Yet, how do I explain this beautiful feeling that has come over me? I desired this in my life.

Was I being tormented and punished? Is Jesus for real? He is the only one who paid a price at Calvary. I had learned this at Sunday School. I just didn't understand how He paid the price or what did He have to pay in full?

I answered the voice I heard. I said, "Yes, Jesus take me by the hand."

I felt very ill and dizzy. I stood over the kitchen sink. I felt like a hand was going down my throat. I vomited up the pills I had swallowed.

I had an incredible encounter with the Lord at a Christian Camp called Rocky Ridge Ranch. My life was now going to take a turn for the better. I gave my life to the Lord at the age of 14.

I had some great losses in life causing more pain and rejection, but I became a professional at hiding my pain. I knew how to look the part of a person who is set free, but I was slowly dying from within.

I believe Jesus died for my sins. I just didn't believe I could be set free and have peace and joy. I sang about it. I told others about Jesus' love and forgiveness and explained that they can be free. They received their joy, and I was happy for them.

Several years later I was still carrying the weight of these monsters in my life. I was collecting more rejection along the way, and it was pulling me down. I couldn't carry the weight anymore.

This continued through two marriages which led to two bitter divorces. It was two of the most painful experiences I had gone through. With two failed marriages, I felt like I was a failure. The words crept into my mind. I asked myself, "How do you think you will be successful at anything when you don't amount to anything?"

I didn't want anything to do with dating or marriage. It was something I no longer desired. Every kind of relationship, even just regular friendships became unhealthy.

As the years kept going by, I came to the end of ever hoping things would get better. I was right to the extent of becoming homeless, but I didn't give up. I met up with a friend I had known from my childhood. He was homeless and I took him in, thinking I could help him get back on his feet.

He was addicted to crack cocaine and alcohol. Instead of helping him, I partook in his addictions. I had never done this before. Now I was facing a new fear and I had added baggage. To add salt to my wounds I was soon living on the streets as well.

Being homeless I felt alone. A new kind of fear came over me. I had to do what I needed to do, to survive but I still had morals. I knew I could say no when I needed to say it, especially when I had sexual offers given to me to do things that only made me feel sick.

I said "No way! Back off!" I stood my ground.

Some professional businessmen and woman invited me to live with them, but they wanted benefits that suited their sexual fantasies. I turned that down quickly. I had lost my hope and trust in people. I wanted to end the pain, but I was not going to try to take my life again. I just wanted to be free and find real joy.

I remember many times when sleeping in the bushes, crying out loud to God asking Him *How long am I going to have to be punished for making mistakes?* and W*here are you? Did you abandon me like my friends and family?*

I cried. *Well, I don't blame you. I gave up on me a very long time ago.*

I ended up in jail for something I didn't do. Yeah, everyone in jail does the crime but say they never did it. However, that was not my case. A year later I was proved innocent in court.

It was Christmas 2006 December 24th, when I was accused of a crime I could never see myself doing. Even in the state of mind I was in, I could never have done a home invasion. How could I prove my innocence? I didn't exactly have a good reputation. However, hurting or bringing harm to another person or robbing them with any weapon is not who I am.

I was guilty of the sins I committed, such as giving in to addiction and believing a lie that Jesus couldn't set me free from the harm that was done to me.

My depression darkened to a whole new level. I felt I was coming to the end of life. I was lying on the bed in my jail cell, and I said goodbye to my Savior. I figured I was going to hell, where I belonged. I felt like the biggest hypocrite on planet earth because I was a believer but didn't have the peace and joy that Jesus gives.

I laid there until four am. I was staring into the exit light outside the guard's post. There were no more thoughts left racing my mind.

Suddenly, I experienced that presence I had felt once before in the kitchen at my parents' house and a few times while I was on the streets. I never acknowledged it right away. I just laid there emotionless, but the presence of Jesus filled my cell. It grew extremely intense, and Jesus appeared before me. I know it wasn't any hallucinations. I wasn't high on crack. Other than my "stinking thinking" I was in my right mind.

I didn't see his face, but I saw the scars on his hands where he was pierced.

There is always going to be something suddenly happening when Jesus walks into the room. Everything came into alignment. Even those monsters are no match for Jesus. As the Lord spoke softly but with authority and holiness the monsters were bound and gagged. I wasn't aware of it until that moment.

Jesus took me into His arms told me He loves me so much that He left the many to come to me and He said He forgives me. As I wept, I repented once again. He told me I am His child, and He is my friend. He said He has much for me to do as He continues to do His work in me.

He said, "No more do you walk with guilt and shame. You now have three new best friends, Grace, Mercy, and Joy. They will walk with you always."

The next day I was free to leave the jail.

I've been set free! Jesus had mercy on me when I was lost. He left the many to come to me while I was dirty in my sin. He called me His child, His friend. Then He set me free, delivered me from those monsters. He delivered and set me free from crack cocaine.

He filled me with joy, peace, and righteousness. Grace and mercy walk beside me. He has restored my soul and healed my relationships. I've received forgiveness from those whom I have hurt and who hurt me.

He sent the right counselors to help me make healthier choices in life. He is still moving in my life restoring my health.

I have been married to my best friend Brenda 11 years this September. I am truly blessed!

Yes, I still have struggles, but I have a Savior who keeps me from wandering away and being lost in the wilderness.

Most of all he restored my hope. It was never really lost. It was just covered up from lies to throw me off track.

Today I don't wear masks. You just cannot cover joy. Any accomplishments in my life were not by my achievements, but by the grace of God.

My health will one day be restored as well. I have heart issues along with other health problems which put me on a disability. I am learning to eat healthier and make wiser choices.

I don't need approval from others to be accepted. Especially when I am accepted by my Creator and Savior. I measure up nicely in his eyes.

I am confident of this Jesus who began a good work in me. He is faithful to complete His work in me. (Paraphrased Philippians 1:6)

Forgive often, love often and never lose joy.

Author Bio: Michael Lock

Michael Lock is a Christian singer, actor, and author. He lives in Windsor, Ontario Canada with the love of his life Brenda. Michael loves to sing and reach out to the less fortunate. He is outgoing, fun, loving, joyful, friendly and a caring person who loves to make people laugh.

He likes to encourage people who have gone through loss and heartbreak in their lives, because he too has experienced a lot of heartbreak and loss. Jesus has been his anchor in the storms of life. Michael is presently writing an autobiography called, "Caged Bird."

Michael has a powerful testimony of how the Lord delivered him from drug addiction and homelessness, and healed him of depression and insecurities, which is detailed in his upcoming book.

In the Midst of Grief

Written as told by Wendy Jackson

Deep down, I believe the Lord brought me through the grief I felt when my 4 ½ year old son Michael died the night before Christmas Eve. I've always had a strong faith in God.

I had been a fan of stories of missing children, such as the story of Adam Walsh. Adam was a six-year-old boy who went missing in 1981.

Eric Clapton wrote a song called, "Tears in Heaven". This song really touched me. I was so grateful I knew where Michael was… he is in heaven.

I was also grateful that we knew Michael was buried in the grave. We didn't have to spend weeks, months or years trying to find him. My children belong to God, so I knew Michael was in heaven.

One of the most difficult things for me was my second daughter, Manda was born two weeks after Michael's death. I was grieving and I couldn't bond with my newborn baby. For the first six months of her life, my mother cared for her. It took me that long to get out of the fog of grief for Michael enough to care for Manda.

One day when I was reading my Bible, I felt God telling me not to read the Bible anymore. I argued with Him about it. I finally broke down and asked Him why I shouldn't read it anymore. He said, "If you don't believe it there's no sense in reading it."

1 John 4:20 says (paraphrased), *"If you say you love God, but you hate a man, then you are a liar."* Even though I did not hate my daughter I

was not loving her the way I should, and I didn't care. I was in too much pain to think about anything else. I knew God was not one to sit on the fence on love. If you don't love with your whole heart, then you don't love at all.

Then He led me to look up the name of my daughter Amanda. Her name means "worthy to be loved." I realized I wasn't loving my daughter. I had abandoned her, and my mom was looking after her.

I knew in Hebrews 13:5b it reads, (paraphrased) *"It is the Lord who goes before you. He will be with you; He will not leave you or forsake you. Do not fear or be dismayed."* I knew I would not want God to abandon me, His daughter, so why am I abandoning my daughter?

I was a parent doing what I didn't want my Heavenly Father doing to me. I had to give in, I had to push my grief aside, not forget or bury it, but just set it aside long enough to allow God to do His work in me. I knew He would be working even when I could not feel it or want it.

I was emotionally, mentally, spiritually, and physically out of it. I tried to do it on my own, but I knew I couldn't. It was then when God kept telling me, "You have to love me with all your heart, not just the parts you want to love me with. I gave you a child and you are not loving her. If you can't love the people who you can see how can you love me who you can't see?"

Once I surrendered myself to God and His will and His way, I totally turned it over to Him. It was then I was able to love Manda and bond with her. God gave me the bond with Manda.

After Michael died there were some visions and dreams that encouraged us. My oldest daughter, Sarah, kept seeing angels and she had a dream that Michael was waiting at the gate of heaven.

Paraphrased, Revelations 4:1 says, *"Come up here, and I will show you what must happen after this."* I didn't even know about this verse until I had a dream about it. Then I found it in the Bible.

In my dream, I saw Jesus standing beside Michael's bed. I saw Michael's spirit come out of him. I heard Jesus say, "Come hither. I'm going to show you what is here and after."

Jesus took Michael's hand and they floated to the living room where my husband, Dave and I were wrapping Christmas gifts. Michael asked Jesus, "What about my mom and dad?"

Jesus said, "Don't worry. I'm going to take care of them."

I always had a hard time remembering dates due to the pain I was feeling. God gave me ways to honor those days in a special way. The pattern of turning something bad on a date into another big event was a way God has been all along with me. It is a blessing how God knows our every need and has a creative way to show it to us. Romans 8:28 says (paraphrased) *that God has a way to turn things into good.*

For example, Michael died on Dec 23, but it also is the same day my cousin had a baby and my brother's birthday is on Dec 23. April 29 is the day that Michael was buried, and it also happens to be my husband's birthday. My husband's father's and my father's death date were both on March 18, (11 years apart.) So, we can remember our fathers on the same day. He took these important, painful dates and made them in a way that has always been a way for my healing and also as a reminder that He has always been there for me and always will be. God takes care of you even in the midst of Grief. Praise His name!

After Michael's Dad and I broke up, I couldn't date anyone with the name Michael or who had a son named Michael. I had a friend whose son was in Michael's class. The last picture of Michael was with this boy sitting on Santa's lap. I was friends with that boy's mom and she had a baby boy. I noticed that she kept calling him "the baby" instead of using his name. One day I asked her about it. She said, "I don't want to tell you because I don't want to hurt you." She finally told me his name was Michael. After that we continued to be good friends.

Another interesting thing happened at Michael's burial that April. My husband and I both saw a woman dressed in black pushing a 1950's baby carriage. Even when we were at opposite ends of the grave, we could see her. I felt strange because she kept looking at me. Later we asked the other people who were there and nobody else saw her! Dave and I both saw her more than once. Could she have been an angel?

Step-by-step, I could see God was with me through my grief. A popular saying is, "I could never survive if one of my children died," I found out you can go on and you can live life and be happy after your child dies.

Recently, my sister-in-law's daughter committed suicide. I've been able to help her a lot as she's going through her grief. There are a lot of questions that surround suicide. She's asking, "Where is my daughter now? Is she in heaven?"

One year and one day later her mom died. So, she's had a lot of grief to deal with.

It is hard to watch other people who are grieving. I know how hard it is. I'd rather go through it myself than see someone else go through it. Some people hold on to the lies that you will never be happy again. For awhile, I held onto my grief and pain because that's all I had.

Acknowledging that letting it go doesn't mean you're letting your child go. Don't buy into the lie that you must hold onto the negative feelings.

You can go on and live life and be very happy.

That past is one of my stones in the pillar of who I am today. I can help other people who are going through grief, especially other women. It's okay to feel those feelings. It's what makes you strong. Without Michael's death I wouldn't be the person I am today.

One of the hard things for my daughter Manda is she wishes she was born a couple weeks earlier so she could have met her brother, even though she wouldn't remember him. She went through a period where this was very important to her.

My other daughter, Sarah, was angry when her brother died. She was only two years old. She said, "You took my brother away and brought this other child in."

Michael was ripped out of our family and Manda was born two weeks later. It was a lot of stress to help Sarah through her grief while I was grieving.

It was hard to deal with my new life. Two weeks previous, I had two children and was expecting my third child. Then suddenly I only had one child. Another change was that my daughter Sarah was now the oldest child in our family.

There was a period where both my husband and I put things from Michael onto Sarah, like "You're the oldest," We had to remember she was not four years old, she was only two years old.

I've always had a strong commitment to God. At that six-month mark, I wrestled with God like Jacob wrestled with God in the Old Testament. If God didn't have that conversation with me, I wouldn't have a relationship with my daughter Manda.

If I had one thing to say to you as you read this, it would be to allow yourself to grieve. What you're feeling is normal. And don't look at other people because everybody grieves differently. It's okay to cry. And it's okay to laugh. You can move forward. You can be happy again.

Author's Bio: Wendy Jackson

Wendy Jackson was born in Toronto, Ontario and raised in Huntsville, Ontario. Now she resides in London, Ontario with her husband Doug. She has two daughters and a son. She is also blessed with 3 grandchildren who she adores. Names of grandchildren, nicknames in () Amanda had Tyson 11 (Ty), and Paisley (Paypay) 8, and Sarah has Sebastian 8,  (nickname Tiaan). Paisley and Tiaan was born two months apart. When Wendy was younger, she had prayed for twins; God gave them to her in His own blessed way through her two grandchildren being born two months apart.

Wendy enjoys time with her husband, children, grandchildren, and their two toy yorkies. She also enjoys renovating homes.

Wendy owns her business as a real estate investor/landlord. She also helps her husband Doug with his internet business, Countryside Communications by doing admin, accounting, and assisting customers through bookings.

Finding Us

by Amy Thomson

I've had so many people in my life pass away. It's just nuts. I even started to think I was cursed. By the time I was 11, I already thought of myself as a funeral connoisseur, because I had attended so many.

Death happens. A lot sometimes. Some deaths made sense to me and others, not so much. For example, a few of my best friends who were young and healthy died suddenly of natural causes; and my mother died last year in the middle of the night with no prior issues or health conditions that I am aware of. She and I were very close too.

Additionally, this past week marks the eight-year anniversary of a horrific murder that happened in our family. It changed everyone's lives.

You know in the movies, when someone needs to change their flight quickly and it seems effortless? Well…it wasn't like that for us.

We touched down at our stopover destination and turned on our phones. Immediately my boyfriend got a frantic phone call from his mother, telling him that our sister-in-law was dead. She was probably one of the nicest people you'd ever want to meet.

We didn't know anything else. Nobody would tell anyone anything. So of course, we tried everything we could to get on an earlier flight, but we couldn't get one. So, we waited at the airport, trying to figure out what might've happened.

Only hours before this, I had been in my hotel room, and finished writing one of my signature programs, The 30 Days to Happiness Program. It has since been a blessing to many people, myself included.

At that present moment, however, in the airport, even though I was incredibly happy, I was still completely in shock and our lives were about to change drastically.

When we finally got home, we couldn't get into the house because the police had it taped up and under investigation. We also couldn't access our vehicles, computers, or anything that was in the house. Luckily for us, I owned another house, so we had somewhere to stay. The police took care of our pets, which was nice, but the house was turned upside down.

During the investigation, they even used a spray on the walls that didn't really come off, which made it so we had to repaint everything. It was sad. We had just finished getting everything the way we wanted it before our trip, and after that incident, although we painted, we never did put our picture walls back up, and the house never felt like a home again.

When we were allowed back into the house, there were now nine of us, instead of six, and it felt squishy. There was only one bathroom, and everyone was sharing rooms. We did what we could to make the best of the situation and keep peace and harmony within the home. Three weeks later, however, the police had gathered enough irrefutable evidence to come to the house and arrest my brother-in-law for the murder of his recent ex-girlfriend, the mother of his kids, and he was taken away.

Prior to the murder, from what I had seen, he had seemed nice. He always helped people. He even helped me with a large charity event that I held. He was community minded. Because he had done so much for people, almost nobody thought he did it. But those who knew him from his younger years, remembered he had a crazy temper and assumed he did, but that was a side of him I didn't know.

At home, our priorities changed. My boyfriend and I already had four kids. Then suddenly we had two more. I loved them instantly, as if they were my own, and although my boyfriend and I were completely willing to raise them, we didn't end up doing so. His sister moved down from out of town and in with us, to take care of them. She became their guardian.

Unfortunately, the whole atmosphere of our house changed too. My boyfriend's family wanted the TV on all the time, literally. For 24 hours a day, seven days a week, the news and murder shows were blasting loudly throughout the house. The conversations around us were rarely about anything pleasant anymore. It was all about the crazy stuff happening at the jail, the ghetto, or anywhere else that violence, crime, and devastating things existed. It was the complete opposite of what our home was like before.

For awhile, I was able to maintain my peace and happiness and bring it to the kids, to the point where I still felt blissful and brought them a lot of love and light (That was due to my happiness program, for sure)... but over time, I began to feel like I shouldn't be happy. My environment didn't support someone being happy, and I began to feel like there was something wrong with me if I was happy.

My environment wore me down and I decided to leave.

I moved back to my house with my kids and although my boyfriend and I stayed together, things were never the same. For years, conversations continued to be about what was wrong in the world, or who was doing what to who.

We rarely had conversations that brought life and creation to our relationship or lives anymore. And although he didn't talk much about what he felt, I know it really affected him. It took over five years for him to travel with me again.

The murder impacted everybody in different ways. For me, I resisted allowing myself to be completely happy again. I couldn't understand how I might have attracted something like that into my life. And because I couldn't make sense of it, I stopped coaching about the things I thought I knew about happiness, or success or about using the Law of Attraction to create the ideal life.

I mean, I had the ideal life. I had created it. I had attracted it. I had also studied happiness and success for over 20 years at that time. I knew what I was talking about... and still... Why did this happen? I seriously couldn't make sense of it.

In fact, after that incident my thoughts drastically changed. I've done a lot of healing, but I definitely still need to do some more clearing work because even now, I check behind the gate when I come home to make sure there's not someone there with a knife. We're still in the same house (I moved back in a couple of years ago), and my boyfriend has had no desire to leave, but we probably should've left years ago.

So, it impacted my whole career, my finances, my confidence, my relationships, my perception of the world, and most of all it impacted the people I love the most.

It's crazy how one event can have such a profound affect on others with so many ripple effects.

Let's talk about my kids, for example. They were terrified, but they didn't talk about it for a long time.

My kids were trying to be there for and support the other kids, but the other kids had professional counselors and therapists. They had charities set up for them. They had many things to help them because they were the ones who suddenly were without a mom or a dad; one was dead and the other in jail, and that would've been a horrendous situation to be in.

My kids, on the other hand, were there through the whole thing, and dealing with their own trauma, but they didn't have any additional supports other than the ones I could get them into, which usually had incredibly long wait lists, or incredibly high fees, which I couldn't afford at the time. They did still have their parents though.

When I did finally get my kids into counseling therapy, it backfired. It didn't work. It wasn't the right match for them with the people. One of my kids even got a little aggressive when I tried to take them for therapy, which was very uncharacteristic for them. This was what also led me into getting trained in trauma and parenting kids with trauma.

To sum it up, what ended up happening was my kids became very afraid of the other people in my boyfriend's family and of my boyfriend himself.

They started staying in their rooms all the time. They were terrified to come out. They wouldn't even come out for necessities of life. They hid a lot of food and became pack rats. It was messy. They got really depressed. Essentially, they lost their freedom, joy, and their interest in life completely. Both of my kids became suicidal, and it was a challenge getting them through those rough times.

One of my kids barely slept for years. He became incredibly vigilant because he was worried that my boyfriend would kill me, so he only slept for a couple of minutes at a time, and never a deep sleep. Eventually, it developed into a lot of mental health issues. Sleep is important. He also wouldn't cry, and he wouldn't talk about what was going on, because he saw it as a weakness. He needed to be strong for me.

When he finally did talk about it, the floodgates opened, and he could let it all out. At first, he talked with me. Then he talked with me and my boyfriend. We were able to help him see that my boyfriend and his brother are two different people. Even though they may be genetically alike, having the same parents, they are different people. My son felt he needed to be on guard at all times and ready to protect me and his sister. It was such a relief when we could finally talk about things, get them sorted out and release some of that thinking.

You know, I think back to when my kids were younger. They had so much joy and pleasure. Lots of laughter, curiosity, and wonder. And it angers me that things have changed so much.

My daughter was so carefree and full of life. She looked forward to every day and had so much fun. She doesn't remember that. She pretty much just remembers the challenges we had and the struggles. So, she asks me sometimes, "Why didn't you abort me? You know I don't want to be here."

Of course, the first feeling I get when she asks me that is the 'Mom Guilt'. That's the feeling of questioning if I made the right decisions and judging how I've been as a parent.

But once that shows up, I turn it back to her and say, "Well, honey...Here's the thing: Even if you left this life, what's to say you're not just going to come back and have to relive it over and over again until you get it right? You might as well do your best now, and enjoy yourself, right?"

My son also used to be really carefree, and at times is beginning to rediscover that. He was born 13 weeks premature and also had a head injury early on, so he had several medical conditions too, which was difficult. We were at the hospital a lot for many years. When it comes to learning, things became very challenging (after the head injury), and he's continuing to develop himself, despite everything.

Luckily, he's done some personal development and communication training, so he has begun to stand in his own power and take charge of his own life. It's helped a lot. That training has been super important because he's also autistic and transgender.

People with autism and those who are transgender are often targets of bullies and abuse. In fact, many transgender people get attacked, beaten, or killed just because they're trying to be on the outside who they are mentally, emotionally, and spiritually on the inside.

The statistics are a very concerning thing as a parent, yet at the same time, do I really want my son to go through his whole life hating himself because of the body he was born into? No! In fact, I want him to be happy and comfortable in his own skin. And he wants that too.

To someone who doesn't understand what it's like to wake up in a body that doesn't feel like theirs, they'd never understand. And for people who would do whatever it takes to be able to be their true selves, they will understand.

Sidenote: To anyone who criticizes, bullies or judges people for thinking or being 'different', please stop. It does no good for anyone. In fact, it hurts people. AND HURT PEOPLE, HURT PEOPLE.

Have you noticed the amount of murders and suicides that have happened over the past few years? My small family has been closely affected by 6 of them, and that's in Canada... where we don't have guns everywhere and we have a pretty safe environment.

So, what's it going to take for us to shift things? I know it's not just me that's been going through these things. I interviewed a friend who owns the largest private wealth company in Canada for my show a few weeks ago, and he said he's been to 3 funerals for suicides recently.

There's almost a culture now where suicide is becoming normal. It's NOT NORMAL. It's a CLEAR SIGN that something needs to change. If I'm being honest, my biggest grief is knowing that I could've done something earlier and helped more people, because I have the skills and knowledge, but I wasn't able to do it then.

When my kids were going through their dark days, I was so desperately trying to keep on top of my career and finances, while also trying to be the best parent and be there for them fully... but I couldn't be at my best everywhere, especially because my worry for them was so great.

I learned that when one person in a family is suffering, the others suffer too, even if they don't fully acknowledge it. When that one person gets medication or support from a therapist, the other people in the family are still impacted and often worried, which doesn't help anyone. It actually creates a space for them to stay in that worried and concerned energy.

The process with my own kids helped me discover that a family can create a healing journey for themselves and each other where each person can choose their own healing path from a series of modalities and personal interests (instead of thinking they 'know what's best' for each other). By practicing communication and supporting each other on their own authentic personal growth and self-expression journey, things become calmer, more enjoyable, and more manageable over time.

We needed to give each other the space, time, support, and faith to rediscover ourselves and grow. We're still doing that, and things continue to get better.

The cool thing is, I've been playing guitar and singing again. I've been playing piano and creating art again. I've been playing games, hula-hooping, going out more, and I've even booked trips. My boyfriend and I are going back to Vegas! It's going to be our first trip back there since the murder! I'm excited and also hoping it will give us closure.

I'm ready for a new chapter in my life. With both of my parents gone (bless their beautiful souls) and many of the key influencers in my life too, it's time for me to step into my own power. After all, I always had different views on how to do things than most people anyway.

I'm finally scaling that company I started. I found a mentor and have shifted my focus to serving large corporations and organizations, instead of just selling to consumers. By serving the people in large organizations, I can also provide value to their families and loved ones as well. There is no sense in working just with the organization when the people in it have extensions of themselves elsewhere.

People should be able to thrive personally and professionally, and know everyone's in the right places, doing their best work, in environments that really support who they are.

My training programs and products bring authenticity, communication, alignment, purpose, strategy, skill-development, collaboration, creativity, visioning, team building, fun, and cohesion to companies and their families.

In a nutshell, I help things work when they don't, and make them work even better when they do, creating cultures where people can thrive.

Thanks for reading through my story. I hope you found value in it. :)

Here Are A Few Things That Helped Me Through My Grief:

The 30 Days To Happiness Program
3 Things That Can Make Me Happy Now (Simple, Effective Technique)
Sharing A Bit Of My Story In This Book
Making Falling In Love With Myself A Priority
Choosing To Have Faith That My Kids Would Be Okay (And Seeing Them As The Powerful, Amazing People They Are)
Developing Myself Personally & Professionally
Taking TECH-FREE Days and getting into nature, or making my home feel better, without any distractions from the outside world
Learning to let go of my 'Lower Self' thinking
Writing, Making Art, Playing Music
Reigniting My Relationship
Allowing Myself To Dream & Have Fun Again
Getting Back Into My Work & Making A Difference For Others
Creating a YouTube channel for Happiness & Success

Author Bio: Amy Thomson
Happiness & Success Expert
Executive, Business & Corporate Trainer/ Coach, Spiritual & Healing Artist

My background is in Project Management, Training and Development, Mind & Consciousness, Business, Sales & Marketing, Metaphysics, Channeling, Writing & Publishing, and Art & Design.

Some of my accomplishments include:
- Top 40 Under 40 Business Award Winner
- Certified Life Coach, High Ticket Sales Coach & Project Manager
- Multi-International Best-Selling Author & Artist 25+ Years Study & Experience in Mental Health, Mind/Body Connection, Metaphysics, Happiness & Success, Spiritual Laws
- Honours in Project Management, Professional Writing, and Art & Design
- Team, Management and Leadership Program (Team 2 Alumni)
- Trauma Trained Parenting Certification
- Think & Grow Rich Institute & The Science of Success Graduate
- Nearly 20 Years As An Entrepreneur
- Certified High-Ticket Closer & High-Ticket Coach
- Mentored In Business By Dan Lok and Coached In Marketing by Alex Mandossian
- Co-author of the book (Journeys to Success 2) foreworded by Bob Proctor
- Creator of Multiple International Award-Winning Brands & Events
- Founder of The Creative Collaboration Summit
- 25+ Years In Teaching/ Coaching/ Mentoring Roles
- Personally Trained & Developed Entrepreneurs in 50+ Countries
- Helped Thousands of People Achieve Success With Their Dreams & Goals

"Yesterday I was clever, so I wanted to change the world. Today, I am wise so I am changing myself." ~Rumi

Email: Success@WhereDreamsConnect.com

https://www.wheredreamsconnect.com/creative-collaboration-summit

https://www.amythomson.vip/

EPILOGUE

Written by Tammy Leigh Robinson

As I was in the middle of preparing this book, I suddenly found myself in the midst of grief again. Five years ago, my husband Keith and I moved from Ontario to New Brunswick. Keith's Mum wasn't well. She was homebound on oxygen 24/7. We moved to help her with her errands and enjoy the last years of her life.

The plan was to live in NB for three to five years (that's how long we expected her to live) then we would move back to Ontario. The first few years were difficult for me because I missed my three grown children, who lived in Ontario. I was grieving them as well as the friendships I had left behind. Of course, with technology we can stay in touch, but it's not the same as being in person.

Last summer when we went "home" to Ontario for a visit both my husband and I agreed the beautiful Niagara region no longer felt like "home". Yet, when we were on our return trip to New Brunswick it felt like we were going "home." We didn't talk about it very much, but both of us felt after his Mum's passing, we would continue living in New Brunswick.

In the meantime, one of my daughters moved to Nova Scotia. She and her husband are now a three-hour drive away. We've been able to see much more of them since they moved. It has been very refreshing. Julie and I even went on a Girls Only Getaway together in NS where we worked on Christmas crafts with a group of crafty women.

The Saturday after our weekend away Keith's Mum died. Although she had been slowly dying for years, when the time came, she went relatively quickly. We got the call that she was doing poorly on Saturday afternoon. She died that night.

With increasing fluid on her lungs, Mum had a hard time breathing. She was semi-conscious due to the morphine. Each of the family members took turns sitting by her side and holding her hand. It was beautiful to see the love she had for each one of us.

As it got later in the evening Keith's brother went home. We didn't think she was going to pass that night. A short time later Keith and I decided to go home. As I leaned over to kiss her cheek and tell her I loved her she didn't respond.

I had an inner feeling that we shouldn't go because she may be dying soon. Unfortunately, I ignored the feeling and proceeded to go home. We live a 30-minute drive away. As soon as we arrived home, we got the call that she had passed.

As much as we'd been expecting it for five years, I was shocked that she was actually gone! I wished we had stayed with her. Later I came to terms with the fact that she died the way she wanted to die... at home. She had her time with each family member, and she simply went to sleep in her chair and didn't wake up.

It was peaceful.

Keith and I drove back to her house. We wanted to say our final good-bye to her. When we arrived the rest of the family gave us a few minutes alone with her. I immediately went to my knees and buried my head in her chest. I bawled. I remember saying, "You were the best Mother-in-law I could have asked for! Thank you for your love! I love you so much!" I'm glad we had the chance to do that. It made the next few days a tiny bit easier because I felt I had closure.

Ever since my daughter Wendy died, I've said that the hardest time for me was after the funeral when everyone went back to their "normal lives", and I was left having to find a new normal with a huge hole in my life.

It was the same with Keith's Mum... yet it was also different. With Wendy I had her every day and she completely relied on my husband and I for everything. With Mum, it was one or two days a week of driving the half hour to Woodstock to do errands and have a visit.

So, we had to find a "new normal", but it wasn't as much of a daily impact. Don't get me wrong. We were still grieving. It was still heart-breaking and hard. We missed her so much! I found I wasn't angry. Mum had lived a full and beautiful life. Everyone who knew her loved her. She was the most generous person I know. She "called a spade a spade". She was a wealth of wisdom and she loved sharing her wisdom as well as her stories.

For me the thing about grieving Mum was that I felt depression and loneliness. I missed our visits with her. So many times, I thought of asking Keith, "Are you going to see Mum today?" or "Was that Mum on the phone?" It takes awhile for the truth to sink in.

There was a similarity in Mum's and Wendy's passing. Both of them were my purpose in life. Wendy was obvious because she was a baby and completely relied on me. With Mum our purpose in moving to NB was for her. As I mentioned our original plan was to move back to Ontario after her estate was settled. I also mentioned last summer we decided not to do that.

So, what were we supposed to do now? We obviously weren't going to make any major decisions right away, but I'm a purpose-oriented and goal-oriented person. I have to know where I'm heading. Were we going to stay in Nackawic? Or would we move somewhere new?

Since we'd agreed not to move back to Ontario, I began to think maybe we should move to Moncton. Then we'd only be an hour away from Julie and Chad. I didn't want to live in NS and neither did Keith. I began to think about it a lot and I even looked at real estate prices.

I felt myself sliding into depression. I was floundering. I felt lost. I kept asking myself, "What now?"

We joked that we had nothing holding us to anywhere, so we could even move to Ireland if we wanted to. We all know I wouldn't want to be that far away from my kids, but it felt like we had so many options –too many options. I felt like we didn't belong anywhere. While Nackawic is technically "home" it ceased to feel like home.

I struggled for a couple months. Christmas came and went with much less enthusiasm than I usually had. I barely even put up the tree. I felt so dead inside.

I knew I needed some direction. I needed to know what our goals were. What was my purpose now? Even though I had Keith and our two international students that we host, I felt alone. I spent time with friends and going to church, but I felt alone.

I knew Keith felt like me. I don't think his grief was as much about his purpose in life but was more about the fact that now both of his parents were dead. I'm so grateful that I have both my parents still living. I had thought I'd feel better if I could go to their house for Christmas but that didn't work out. For the first time in over 26 years, I thought about moving back to Muskoka. It was a very brief thought, but it came to my mind as an option.

In sales, they say not to offer too many options because most people won't choose anything if there are too many options. I felt I had too many options, and none of them felt like the right thing.

I took a break from the Stories of Good Grief project in December – partly because of Christmas, but mostly because I was drowning in my own grief. How was I supposed to share positive coping mechanisms for grief when I was struggling myself?

Finally, one Sunday in January the message at church really resonated with me. Keith and I had a great talk afterwards. He shared that he had no plans to move any time soon. Usually, I react quickly to major statements like that.

However, this Sunday, I let it sink in. I asked myself, "What would it look like to stay where we are indefinitely?"

Suddenly, a peace filled my being. I realized we were "home". We had created a place in our small town of Nackawic and in our Journey church family. All my children were healthy and had their own places in their communities, so they didn't "need" us to move closer to them.

I asked myself, "If we stay here, what will my purpose in life be?" The answer was almost immediate. I would focus on being a clear reflection of the unconditional love of Jesus Christ especially to my husband, children, students, and my friends.

Wow! The peace I felt is indescribable! I felt secure again. I felt that I "belong" here. I have a clear direction. I can focus on my relationships and my writing business.

I was so relieved that hope finally came shining through. Does that mean we're going to stay here forever? Who knows? I don't know. I only know that for right now we are where we want to be and where we're meant to be. Finally, I've found a new reality.

I felt like the sun was shining brightly but was hidden by thick black clouds. Suddenly, the clouds moved, and the sun is shining brightly once again.

The important part for me in this season of grief was to get in touch with my feelings. Ask the tough questions. And I reached out to my loved ones. I shared my feelings, including my misgivings.

One quote that inspires me to have a positive perspective is something Tony Robbins often says, "Life happens FOR you not TO you."

I hope when you have read these stories that you have found some ideas and suggestions that help you through your season of grief. We know the grief never ends, but it changes –the sharpness of the pain eases after some time goes by.

More Stories of Good Grief

As you've read this book, are you thinking about your own grief story? Perhaps you are wondering if your story would encourage people. We invite you to share your story of grief with us for possible future publication.

Please send an email to: admin@TammyRobinsonAuthor.com

About the Author

Tammy lives with her soulmate and husband Keith in picturesque Nackawic, New Brunswick home of the world's largest axe. Mother of three, an angel in heaven, and a stepson; Grammy to her grand-daughter and great grand-son, Tammy loves spending time with her family and friends.

Author of the NAMELESS Trilogy, Tammy has written the first two books in the historical fiction series as well as a Devotional Journal titled <u>Promises From God</u>.

Through Tammy's many life experiences, she has become a strong and courageous woman who wholly believes we can do all things through God who gives us strength.

Tammy enjoys speaking opportunities where she can share her story with others, encouraging them to keep going and never give up.

Suicide awareness is near and dear to Tammy's heart as she almost died from her last suicide attempt, many years ago. She has realized that suicide is a permanent solution for a temporary problem.

She has also learned the importance of communicating her feelings to others to get their perspective on any given situation. She feels strongly that it is sometimes impossible to see the forest through the trees. Getting someone else's opinion can create some wonderful new ideas.

The latest addition to their family is Syndi, a golden doodle puppy, who has provided love and support to Tammy and Keith.

Manufactured by Amazon.ca
Bolton, ON